King County Collects

TREASURES OF OUR
HISTORICAL ORGANIZATIONS

Foreword by John Chaney

Chapter commentaries by Dick Wagner, Ralph Munro, Lawrence Kreisman,
Mary T. Henry, Alan Stein, Jim Compton, Patricia Filer, Olaf Kvamme,
Leonard Garfield, Paula Becker, Jim Kelly, and Charles Payton

Photos assembled from the collections of members of the
Association of King County Historical Organizations
(AKCHO) - details in Index of Photos at end of book

Created by AKCHO, Seattle, Washington
Distribution by University of Washington Press

Edition One – October, 2013

## Copyright and Fair Use

The images in this book are drawn from the collections of 61 historical organizations in King County, Washington, known as the Association of King County HIstorical Organizations (AKCHO).

With appropriate permission, each organization would be happy to provide reasonably priced reproductions of their photographs for your personal or commercial use. The income from these lab fees and use fees helps to support our ongoing efforts to preserve and make accessible these primary source documents of King County history.

Copyright protection is provided by laws of the United States and other countries to the creators of "original works of authorship" including literary, dramatic, artistic, musical, and certain other intellectual works. This book is such a work and is protected by copyright law. United States Copyright Law (Title 17, U.S.C.) restricts unauthorized use of copyrighted material; potential users must obtain permission from the copyright holder.

The nature of historical archival photograph collections means that copyright or other information about restrictions may be difficult or even impossible to determine. Please contact the owning repository if you have additional information regarding the images contained herein.

## Fair Use

The doctrine of fair use allows limited use of copyrighted material without permission from the copyright holder. Fair use includes comment, criticism, teaching, and private scholarship. The organizations featured in this book welcome fair use of its contents. All other uses require written permission from the owning institution.

AKCHO
PO Box 3257
Seattle, WA 98114
www.akcho.org

Distributed by
University of Washington Press
P.O. Box 50096
Seattle, WA 98145-5096
www.washington.edu/uwpress

# Table of Contents

# Foreword

**Enjoy, it is our pleasure to share with you!**

King County has a rich heritage. Our historical organizations are the repositories of our collective past and with this volume we offer a tiny glimpse of those treasures for your viewing. This book represents the work of volunteers and staff of heritage organizations around King County and the financial support of individuals, organizations and especially 4Culture. Without this group effort this work would not have been possible.

**Visit, we welcome you!**

A picture may tell the story of a thousand words but nothing can replace the experience of the original. There is a special understanding of the past that flows from the authentic to you. Follow your interests and visit a local historical organization, see how our collected treasures tell a story of triumph and loss, a story of struggle and success, a story saved from being forgotten and now shared with us all.

**Join in, help keep our history alive!**

History is a living thing. We are all a part of our collective past and now we must move together into our future. Be an active part of sharing our collective story. Today there are parts of our past that need to recorded, preserved and passed on. Can you help record the memories of an elder for future generations? Do you hold a story that was entrusted to you and should be preserved? There are objects stored away that could become a part of our shared history. Will you consider sharing with your neighbors and community?

**Please support King County heritage organizations in their mission!**

Our historical organizations, large and small, have a special role in helping us all understand our past. Thousands of volunteer hours are invested in preserving and sharing with our King County citizens and visitors. Consider becoming a volunteer. Renew or become a member of one or more organizations. They will welcome your help and membership support. If you have the means please consider a gift, large or small. Preserving our collective history is a big project and you can help keep the lights on, refurbish an exhibit or help support programs that engage young people with history. Consider sharing your talents and treasure to keep our past alive. Your investment will help us all go together into our future.

**John Chaney**
*December, 2012*
*President, Association of King County Historical Organizations*

# Acknowledgements

From the very beginning, this innovative anthology with a working title of "King County Collects" was the brainchild of Lorraine McConaghy, PhD, Public Historian with the Museum of History & Industry (MOHAI). To her and to MOHAI we owe a large debt of gratitude. Dr. McConaghy carefully shepherded the early stages of the book. She devised the book's chapters to illuminate King County's historical development through the holdings of heritage organizations, and created a work plan for collecting images of those materials that would involve every AKCHO organizational member. She arranged for premier photographer Richard Nicol to capture the images, and traveled with him to each venue, personally selecting the artifacts, ephemera and photos that would best represent the breadth of King County historical organizations' collections.

Museum of History & Industry Executive Director Leonard Garfield believed in the project and the importance of MOHAI's participation in it, and generously allocated time for Dr. McConaghy to work on the book, along with that of other employees and volunteers who helped record and organize the thousands of resulting slides. MOHAI generously stored the slides and data for nearly the entire length of the project. The devoted expertise of Dr. McConaghy, the support and partnership of Leonard Garfield and MOHAI, and the beautiful photography of Richard Nicol were the driving forces that launched the compilation. Such projects also need support in the form of funding. 4Culture, the Cultural Development Authority of King County, provided grants that were instrumental in completing the photography, design and publishing of the book.

The project, the original impetus for which was the Sesquicentennial of King County, has spanned a little more than a decade, and has even generated an on-line venture, spearheaded once again by Lorraine McConaghy and MOHAI in partnership with the University of Washington Libraries Special Collections. The King County Collects images were paired with the King County Snapshots website hosted by the University of Washington, and with many thanks to the University of Washington, in the person of Ann Lally and other UW staff, the AKCHO slides were scanned as part of the on-line project. This made the images immediately accessible to the general public, and also resulted in providing the AKCHO publication project with the digital images necessary for today's publication requirements. After a spreadsheet of the images was prepared, and captions for the on-line project were entered by MOHAI staff at the direction of Dr. McConaghy, the project slides were transferred to the Eastside Heritage Center. Grateful thanks to EHC Director Heather Trescases and that organization for the generous offer to handle and store the large collection of slides.

Many have contributed toward the completion of the book. Dr. McConaghy wrote the initial captions for the first two chapters, and continued to guide the process. It was her suggestion that people prominent in the field of our regional history write the introductions for each chapter. Twelve heritage specialists were asked, and twelve gave positive responses. We sincerely thank Dick Wagner, Ralph Munro, Lawrence Kreisman, Mary T. Henry, Alan Stein, Jim Compton, Patricia Filer, Olaf Kvamme, Leonard Garfield, Paula Becker, Jim Kelly and Charles Payton for their thoughtful discourse on the subject matter of their assigned chapters. Vicki Stiles next took up the call for editing and, with Corey Fish, kept the ball rolling on photos and captions. We are very grateful to Corey Fish for his time, expertise and willingness to work with us, and for his captivating layout and design. He has remained on the project, and given it the fine quality that it deserves. As we came into the home stretch, Barbara McMichael and Alice Winship gave the editing enormous attention and fine-tuning, bringing it all together.

There have been several AKCHO boards during the space of the King County Collects project, of which all members have moved the project along during their terms. That means several presidents, and several treasurers, all of whom have stood by the project throughout its life. Each one deserves thanks for holding fast, but a special thank you must go to Bob Fisher, who, as the final treasurer handling the project funds and grants, must tie it all together and wind things up. We very much appreciate his deft management, knowing that everything will be balanced at the end.

Finally, very sincere thanks to all of the participating organizations for which this project was conceived, and without which the project could not exist. You are the keepers of the history of our great King County region, and you are the substance of this cooperative effort. Together with all those who had a hand in bringing this book about, you make a compelling case for the preservation of our most valuable cultural resource, our heritage.

**Sesquicentennial Leadership Gifts - $5,000 and Up**
4Culture
Lorraine and Rob McConaghy
Museum of History & Industry
King County Landmarks and Heritage Commission

**Legacy Donors - $1,000 to $4,999**
King County
King County Executive Ron Sims
King County Council
Greg Nickels
Larry Phillips
Louise Miller
Larry Gossett
David Irons
Peter von Reichbauer
Rob McKenna
Dwight Pelz
Jane Hague
Cynthia Sullivan
Kent Pullen
Maggi Fimia
Les Thomas
City of Seattle
Mayor Paul Schell
Seattle City Council
Heidi Wills

Judy Nicastro
Peter Steinbrueck
Richard Conlin
Richard McIver
Jan Drago
Nick Licata
Margaret Pageler
Jim Compton

**Other Legacy Donors:**

**AKCHO Board Members**
Leonard Garfield
Bob Gruhn
Jim Kelly
Karen Klett
Leon Leeds
Charles Payton
Ethel Telban
Marcie Williams

**Organizations**
Eastside Heritage Center
Experience Music Project
Nordic Heritage Museum
Shoreline Historical Museum
White River Valley Museum

# chapter one

# Managing the Natural World

*by Dick Wagner*

King County is a geographic and biologic medley of snow-capped mountains, misty rain forests, countless rivers and lakes and an inland sea. There is a hodgepodge of animals including whales, bears, elk, otters, beavers, mountain lions, sea lions, eagles, and great blue herons. Its diverse natural elements are entwined in a complex, self-sustaining order. The threads of its bountiful tapestry began

This 14-foot model accurately depicts HMS *Discovery*, the ship that Captain George Vancouver sailed from England to explore the far side of the world. Duwamish oral tradition maintains that a very young Chief Seattle witnessed *Discovery's* arrival on Puget Sound. On May 19, 1792, Vancouver dispatched Lieutenant Peter Puget and Master Joseph Whidbey to conduct a survey of local waters. The Vancouver expedition charted and renamed numerous landmarks, including Mt. Rainier, Whidbey Island, and of course, Puget Sound. These names replaced those of the Native geography. Discovery Modelers Education Center. ▼

◄ Snoqualmie Falls and the Snoqualmie Valley were photographed by Ellis. The Snoqualmie people held these magnificent falls to be sacred. King County communities have often experienced the mighty power of our regional rivers, swollen with rain and snowmelt. Snoqualmie Valley Historical Society.

◄ This canoe was paddled down a flooded Kent street. During the Great Flood of 1906, the Kent Valley turned into a giant lake as rivers overflowed their banks and flood water rose up to two feet in some houses. Greater Kent Historical Society.

to weave together about 13,000 years ago when the 3,000-foot-deep Vashon glacier retreated. In 1792 Britain sent the ships *Discovery* and *Chatham*, under the command of George Vancouver, to survey the Northwest coast. Vancouver's charts, from the Columbia River to Anchorage, Alaska, were the first ever of the coast. He found the land, including Puget Sound, to be unlikely for European settlement because of the impenetrable forests and undergrowth. Vancouver envisioned a new world that replicated 18th-century farms with classic stone houses and grassy plains with sheep grazing.

Unfortunately, after thousands of years of primal coordination that perfectly aligned the environment that Vancouver reported, it is no longer the same. The main reason for the change is human impact. In 1792 there were about two thousand natives in King County. Now there are over a million diverse residents. The permanent establishment of newcomers began with the Denny party: 12 adults and 12 children, immigrants from Illinois who established a village at Alki Point in 1851.

▲ Two years before this real estate map was published, Washington achieved statehood and Seattle burned to the ground. Here, in this 1891 map of Seattle, we see the city rebuilt, risen from the ashes. Six years later, in 1897, Seattle really began to boom, outfitting and entertaining would-be miners headed north to pan for gold. Seattle Public Library.

RATTLESNAKE LAKE FLOOD AT CEDAR FALLS WN 1915

▲ As Seattle grew, clean drinking water became a critical public health issue. The creation of the Cedar River watershed caused dramatic changes in King County. Here, as shown in a 1915 photo, construction of a massive dam on the river slowly flooded the valley, drowning the town of Cedar Falls under Rattlesnake Lake. Snoqualmie Valley Historical Society.

Cedar River pipeline No. 1 was photographed under construction, with a crew hauling pipe uphill east of Renton in 1900. Seattle's water system was the city's first municipally-owned utility. Numerous King County towns were abandoned within the Cedar River watershed to keep the city's drinking water pure. Seattle Municipal Archives. ▼

◄ This photo, taken in 1929 at Fifth Avenue between Lenora and Blanchard, shows the first Denny Hill regrade in the foreground and the object of the second regrade in the background. Seattle engineers dramatically reshaped the contours of the land on which downtown Seattle was situated, leveling hills, diverting streams and filling the tide flats. Seattle Municipal Archives.

Almost immediately the tall, straight Douglas Fir and Red Cedar trees were cut and exported by ship to San Francisco for pilings. Within a year of arrival the little outpost had a steam-powered sawmill and began shipping out sawn timbers. The forests soon became stump farms. The new occupants of King County had vision and determination to shape a new environment that would fit their enterprising dreams. Even after a devastating fire in 1889 razed much of the wood-built city, the Seattle of 1891 was thriving with stores, industries, residences, schools and churches on the hills above the bay. The wharfs were always filled with sail and steam commercial vessels, passenger ferries and even yachts. The Northern Pacific transcontinental line had a terminal in Seattle, stimulating trade to and from the eastern interior and the Pacific Rim.

Seattle's development reached its "City Beautiful" status after the Yukon Gold Rush which began when the "ton of gold" was brought to Seattle in 1897. The gold rush was a windfall for all the entrepreneurs in town, from those who supplied the goods needed by the miners, to the boat builders and operators that brought the miners to Alaska.

After the Gold Rush, a new population of middle class appeared and they stimulated a housing boom. The new economy made social change and

▲ This postcard by C. B. Bussell was a real estate promotion of "Tide Lands." The filling of Elliott Bay's tidelands along Seattle's southern shore opened new land to development of every sort. Speculators and industrialists were encouraged to invest in this acreage. Washington State Historical Society.

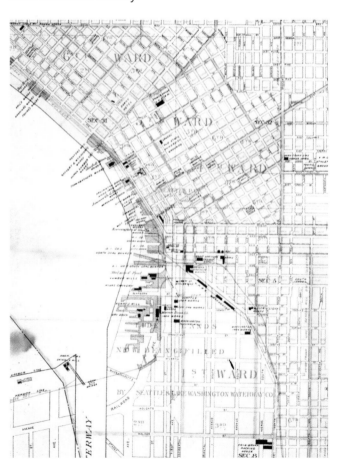

▲ Seattle tidelands maps, 1908, from *Baist's Real Estate Atlas of Surveys of Seattle, Wash.* University of Washington Libraries.

This view of Lake Washington was taken from Mt. Baker Park Boulevard in 1914 by Asahel Curtis. Lake Washington was renamed on July 4, 1854, by settler Thomas Mercer; local Duwamish people had called it "Big Lake" in their language to distinguish it from smaller Lake Union. Lake Sammamish, Lake Washington and Lake Union – as well as the rivers that threaded King County – offered water highways to canoes and steamers, but they placed impediments in the way of wheeled transportation. Washington State Historical Society. ▼

At the same holiday picnic where he renamed Lake Washington, Mercer also renamed Lake Union, dreaming of a future "union" between the freshwater of Lake Washington and the saltwater of Shilshole Bay. It took more than 60 years to accomplish his vision, as shown in this 1920 plat map of Lake Union and Montlake. National Archives and Records Administration. ▶

environmental change. The removal of Denny Hill, rising 600 feet over the shore of Elliott Bay in the early 1900s, was one of those ingenious why-not ideas of King County. Denny Hill was one of Seattle's original seven. If that hill weren't there, Seattleites thought, their expanding commercial and industrial business could more easily be accommodated. So they rigged up high-pressure hoses, pumping the water from Puget Sound to wash the hill into the bay, and created the Denny Regrade. The Regrade remained a lightly used parking lot until after the 1962 Seattle World's Fair when its potential was recognized and the condos, restaurants and night clubs sprang forth.

Tides and rivers are important factors in the environment of Puget Sound, and in some cases are dominant. There is an average of 12 feet between high and low tides which should be well known by clam diggers, shellfish harvesters, and the crew of vessels tied to a wharf. Tidal currents get so violent in narrow passages that whirlpools can suck down boats. Rivers are fed by the snow fields in the mountains. Water is non-compressible. It will push very hard to get out of a container that is too small. In the springtime the migrating waterfowl arrive, the daffodils bloom and the floods flood. An extra-high tide or significant snow melt will turn a paved street into a flowing stream, allowing shopping by canoe or migration by salmon. Traffic lights can be ignored. The control of water flow may be our biggest and longest ongoing challenge.

Real estate promotion was one of the most vital industries in the first century of the county's development. Then, there were more trees than people. The developers were in the money-making game, and to market the primal land, they had to get the people out there. To this end, the developers were the first providers of roads and public transit. They often built amenities such as docks and even parks with bandstands for concerts on summer Sundays. The natural assets that are part of King County are still preserved, more or less, in many parks. For instance, from Mt. Baker Park, planned by the Olmsted

▲ This 1958 pro-vote Metro poster supported passage of a county-wide set of initiatives that included a regional effort to cleanse Lake Washington, which had become badly polluted. As early as 1943, lake beaches were often closed in the summertime because of public health concerns; postwar suburbanization increased this problem. Washington State Archives.

The work to connect Lake Union and Lake Washington began in 1914. The Lake Washington Ship Canal would connect the towns surrounding the shores of Lake Washington with Puget Sound via the Hiram M. Chittenden Locks, which were being built at the same time between Lake Union and Salmon Bay. The price for this feat of engineering would be dear, however. The completed cut caused a permanent lowering of Lake Washington, and while the shores gained additional waterfront property, fisheries were decimated, the Black River all but disappeared, and steamer travel around the lake and up the Sammamish River to Lake Sammamish was no longer possible. Shoreline Historical Museum. ▼

A house on the flooded Snoqualmie River was photographed in 1892 by Darius Kinsey. Snoqualmie Valley Historical Society. ▶

Brothers, one looks up the long blue trough of Lake Washington and toward the Cascade Mountains beyond. On a clear day one can see Mt. Rainier to the south and Mt. Baker to the north, almost at the Canadian border.

The three-mile-long floating bridge across Lake Washington is a good example of how we manage our environment and of the can-do spirit of the region. By 1940, Seattle was a substantial metropolitan city on the west side of Lake Washington, while on the east side of Lake Washington were fruit and berry farms. To reach the other side one either drove around the 20-mile-long lake or took a charming pedestrian steam ferry.

Pragmatic engineering rules said that the lake was too wide and too deep (200 feet) for a bridge. Seattle said throw out the rule book and build a bridge that floats. The Eastside now is as popular as Seattle. Homes and commercial structures now stand on the old strawberry fields.

_Dick Wagner and his wife, Colleen, founded The Center for Wooden Boats on Seattle's Lake Union in 1978._

## INFORMATION IN BRIEF

| | |
|---|---|
| Total Project Length | 33,655.76 feet |
| Total Project Cost | *$7,675,688.45 |

* This total does not include costs of right-of-way, engineering and supervision.

### BASIC FINANCING

| | |
|---|---|
| United States P.W.A. Grant | $3,934,875.00 |
| Toll Bridge Revenue Bonds | 5,900,000.00 |

### WORK PROGRAM

| | |
|---|---|
| Construction Work Commenced | Dec. 29, 1938 |
| Date Opened to Traffic | July 2, 1940 |

### FLOATING STRUCTURE

| | |
|---|---|
| Number of Standard Floating Sections | 10 |
| Number of Special Floating Sections | 15 |
| Length of Standard Floating Section | 350 feet |
| Width of Standard Floating Section | 60 feet |
| Depth of Standard Floating Section | 14½ feet |
| Weight of Standard Floating Section | 4,558 tons |
| Height of Roadway Above Water | 7½ feet |
| Height of Rail Above Water | 10½ feet |
| Width of Roadway—4 Traffic Lanes | 45 feet |
| Sidewalks (2) | 4 feet |
| Thickness, Bottom and Outside Walls | 8 inches |
| Thickness, Cell Walls | 6 inches |
| Size of Cell | 14x14x14 feet |
| Number of Cells, Standard Section | 96 |
| Number of Water-tight Compartments, Standard Section | 12 |
| Length of Floating Draw Span | 378 feet |
| Channel Opening | 202 feet |
| Diameter Anchor Cables | 2¾ inches |
| Weight—Type "A" Standard Anchor | 65 tons |
| Total Number of Anchors | 64 |
| Length of Floating Bridge | 6,561 feet |
| Depth of Flotation | 7 feet |
| Maximum Depth of Lake | 210 feet |

## FEATURE FACTS

[1] Largest Floating Structure ever built by man. Weight—approximately 100,000 tons.
[2] First reinforced concrete floating roadway bridge ever built.
[3] Reinforcing steel equal to 700 miles of 1⅛-inch square bars used in pontoon construction.
[4] Cost of floating structure and bridge approaches approximately $500.00 per lineal foot.
[5] Weight of Floating Structure 13 tons per lineal foot.
[6] Total number of cells in floating structure—1900.
[7] An average expenditure of $16,000.00 was made every day over the 18-month construction period, Jan. 1, 1939, to June 30, 1940.
[8] During the entire construction not a single fatality to workmen.
[9] Short wave radio was used in locating the anchors.

### BASIC TOLL:
Passenger Car and driver, 25 cents.

For further information address:
**WASHINGTON TOLL BRIDGE AUTHORITY**
Transportation Building
OLYMPIA, WASHINGTON

Lake Washington
FLOATING BRIDGE
SEATTLE, WASHINGTON

T THING AFLOAT
THE WORLD—
our-lane highway
-and-a-quarter long
ng on a picturesque
nty-two-mile lake

◄ This 1940 brochure for the opening of the I-90 floating bridge is titled "The Biggest Thing Afloat in the World." It promoted the Lacey V. Murrow Memorial Bridge, the first bridge to cross Lake Washington. This great structure proved to be the bridge to the future, displacing the cross-lake ferries and opening the Eastside to suburban residential development. Eastside Heritage Center.

# chapter two

# Peoples of King County

*by Ralph Munro*

The diversity of King County peoples is nothing new. From the earliest days, the area of our state which we now designate as King County has been one of many ethnic and racial backgrounds. Before the arrival of European and Asian settlers, the Native American tribal peoples describe intermarriage with coastal and northern tribes. Then our first non-native explorers, Hawaiians and Sandwich Islanders, came into the mix and it wasn't long after that Europeans and Asians began to flood into the region searching for good farm land and jobs in the many new mills and mines, and on the railroads.

As a child, I remember traveling from Bainbridge Island to Seattle to see my grandparents who lived at the end of the Number 7 bus line through Rainier Valley. We would leave the ferry and walk along the waterfront hearing the banter of the Filipino cannery workers along Alaska Way. As we went through Pioneer Square there were many Native Americans congregated around the giant totems. And then after catching the bus on Third Avenue it was up Jackson Street through Chinatown and into the African American neighborhoods of "upper Jackson." As the bus turned right onto Rainier Avenue, we immediately entered "Garlic Gulch" and

Stone projectiles made by Native people between 5,000 and 8,000 years ago were uncovered from a prehistoric fishing-and-hunting camp at the Marymoor archaeological site on the banks of the Sammamish River in Redmond. Burke Museum of Natural History and Culture ▼

Long cylindrical fish traps such as this were woven of willow withes and were used by Native people to catch steelhead trout in local rivers. White River Valley Museum. ▶

▲ Found on the beaches in the Des Moines area, this collection of Native American stone tools includes a pestle or grinder, and weights to hold a fish net in place in the water. Des Moines Historical Society.

the vast Italian neighborhoods that stretched from Emil Sick's baseball stadium all the way to Columbia City and Pritchard Beach. And then as we climbed the hill toward Prentice Street and the "end of the line" we saw the finely kept homes of Swedes, Norwegians, Scots, Japanese and Germans that overlooked south Lake Washington.

Today much of that area is part of Zip Code 98118; the Italians have moved on, only to be replaced by Vietnamese, Thai and other Southeast Asian families. And now if you look closely, you will see Ethiopians and Somalis moving down the hill from Central Seattle to leave their mark on this remarkable place. The United States Census Bureau has proclaimed Zip Code 98118 to be the most diverse in America. But that's no surprise – just take a walk through Seward Park and listen to the languages being spoken on a Sunday afternoon.

Yes, we are still blessed with diversity of peoples in King County. It has made us a better place. And thank goodness for all the fine museums, archives and historical groups in King County that are preserving this valuable heritage. We are lucky people indeed!

---

*Ralph Munro was the Secretary of State for the State of Washington for 20 years. He has written dozens of articles and papers on the history of people and politics, and is a staunch advocate for local historical organizations. Munro has helped lead the Heritage Caucus in Olympia for the past 30 years and serves as an advocate for historic preservation, civics education and heritage in general. An oft-decorated Scotsman, he is proud of the diversity he helps bring to our state.*

▲ Seattle and the towns of King County are built on Indian ground, secured by treaties hastily negotiated in 1854 and 1855. The Duwamish chief Seattle (Siaʔl) made his mark on the Point Elliott Treaty, concluded at Mukilteo, on January 22, 1855. The portrait of Chief Seattle was painted from a photograph taken in 1865, and documents his commanding presence. Pioneer Association of the State of Washington.

| Date of Arrival. | Vessel's Name. | Tonnage | Built where and when. | Papers. | Master's Name. | Number of Crew | Cargo |
|---|---|---|---|---|---|---|---|
| Nov. 15. 1851 | Brig George Emery | 178 5/95 | Saucy ... 1846 | Coast License | James M. Bachelder | 8 | Merchandise & Ballast |
| " " " | Schooner Exact. | 114 2/95 | Connecticut | Tem Register | Isaiah Folger | six | Ship Stores & Ballast |
| " 28 " | British Steamer Beaver | 207 62/95 | England. | Brit Register | Charles E. Stuart | | Ballast & Ship [Merchandise] |
| " " " | British Brigantine Mary Dare. | 174 81/95 | England. | Brit Register | William A. Mouat | | Merchandise |
| Dec. 10 " | Schooner Damariscove | 102 50/95 | New Castle Maine 1849. | Register | Lafayette Balch | | Trade Goods, Ballast & |
| | Brig Orbit | 154 42/95 | Dorchester Co. Md 1845 | (On my arrival I found the Orbit here undergoing | | | |
| Jan. 9. 1852 | Brig G. W. Kendall | 183 | Booth Bay Maine 1846 | Register | A. B. Gove | 8 | Merchandise & |
| " 20 | British Schooner Alice | 45 93/95 | Vancouver's Isle. 1851 | Brit Register | James Cooper | 5 | Sea Stores & Ballast |
| " 9 | Schooner Susan Sturges | 125 | | Coast License | John C. Huffington | | Merchandise |
| " " | Brig John Davis | 148 | | | George Plummer | | |
| Feb. 3 " | Schooner Damariscove | 102 50/95 | New Castle Maine 1849 | Register | Lafayette Balch | | |
| | Schooner Franklin | 85 74/95 | Belfast. Me. 1850. | License | G. W. Kickham | 5 | |
| " 16 | British Brigantine Mary Dare | 174 81/95 | England | Brit Register | William A. Mouat | 12 | |
| March 1 " | Schooner Mary Taylor | 84 | | Register | H. M. Hutchinson | | Mdz. Mill Irons, Printing Press &c |

▲ The Denny party left Portland for Puget Sound on the schooner *Exact* on November 5, 1851, and landed at Alki Point on November 13. This *Exact* log entry listed the Denny family, who sailed to join the advance party, which included David Denny, Arthur Denny's brother. National Archives and Records Administration.

The party of settlers who camped in the winter rain at Alki Point was led by a young man named Arthur Denny. At 29 years of age, Denny left Illinois with his wife and brother, his father and stepmother, and her extended family. Influenced by the rhetoric of manifest destiny, the Denny party intended to found a city of smokestacks in the far west, at the meeting point of steamships and locomotives. It is appropriate that Arthur Denny was a professional surveyor, accustomed to bringing order and organization to the land. This is his surveyor's compass. Washington State Historical Society. ▶

In the spring of 1852, many of the original Alki settlers relocated to the mudflats of Elliott Bay. Arthur Denny became the leader of the community which would become Seattle. Pioneer Association of the State of Washington. ▶

In 1888, Arthur Denny published *Pioneer Days on Puget Sound.* Denny described his experiences crossing the continent on the Oregon Trail and settling Puget Sound. This first edition of his autobiography was personally inscribed to "A.W. Pray with compliments of Arthur A. Denny." Southwest Seattle Historical Society. ▶

◄ A Native American encampment was photographed on the shore of the Green River in about 1900. Such temporary encampments were set up when local tribes picked hops and berries for settlers – a sideline from their traditional harvest of salmon. White River Valley Museum.

◄ Henry Yesler was born into a German-American community in 1810, and worked his way west, learning the machinist trade in Ohio. He established Puget Sound's first steam-powered sawmill in 1853, turning the wealth of timber into marketable lumber. Yesler lived in a custom-of-country relationship with Susan Suquardle, the Native daughter of a Yesler sawmill foreman, and they had a child together. Sarah Yesler, the industrialist's wife, eventually joined him in Seattle. He served as King County's first auditor, was elected mayor of Seattle, founded Seattle's first water system, and ultimately made his fortune in real estate. Yesler died in 1892. Seattle Public Library.

# Society

Settlers called this woman "Princess Angeline" with both mockery and respect. She was Kick-is-om-lo, the daughter of Seattle (Siʔal), the Duwamish chief for whom the little town on Elliott Bay was named. Her dignity is revealed in this oil painting, done by Jacob Elshin between 1945 and 1950. Museum of History & Industry. ▶

This wood and metal rosary dates to the period 1870 to 1890 and belonged to Princess Angeline. The rosary and basket (see photo, lower right) clearly show her mingling of two worlds as she continued to practice traditional crafts but also adopted the religion of newcomers. Archives of the Archdiocese of Seattle. ▼

Woven of coiled cedar root by Princess ▶ Angeline, the clam basket is contemporary to her rosary. After her father's death in 1866, she lived in a small home on the waterfront, creating these baskets for sale on the streets of Seattle. Baskets such as this were traditionally made by Native women for gathering and food preparation. Burke Museum of Natural History and Culture.

◄ At the turn of the 20th century, German-American Frederick Karl Struve was one of Seattle's most successful and prominent citizens. A real estate business man and banker, Struve was president of Seattle National Bank, and he and his wife Anna Furth Struve moved in the highest circles of Seattle society. This painting of Fredrick K. Struve is undated. Museum of History & Industry.

◄ Born in New York, Robert Moran migrated west and initially worked as an engineer on a Puget Sound steamboat. Moran and his brothers soon opened a shipyard on the Seattle waterfront, which became very successful. Moran was elected mayor of Seattle in 1888 and governed the city during the Great Seattle Fire of 1889. The Moran shipyard was destroyed in the fire but was rebuilt, and successfully launched the battleship *Nebraska* in 1907. Robert and Annie Moran built the beautiful mansion "Rosario" on Orcas Island. This is a painting of Annie Moran. Pioneer Association of the State of Washington.

Built in 1927, Broadmoor was billed as a "country club within the city," but with fortunes lost during the Depression, it wasn't until after World War II that it became an exclusive enclave for the wealthy. This invitation to move to Broadmoor dates to 1929, the year of the great stock market crash. Washington State Historical Society. ▶

BROADMOOR

An Invitation
IS HEREBY EXTENDED TO
*Mr & Mrs Charles A. Musson*
TO BECOME A RESIDENT OWNER AT
BROADMOOR
SEATTLE, WASHINGTON

PUGET MILL COMPANY

▲ Immigrants depended on boarding houses for meals and companionship, and boarding houses were springboards to a job and eventually a home of one's own. Photographed around 1900, this Seattle boarding house was located between Virginia and Stewart on Boren Avenue, in Seattle. Swede-Finn Historical Society.

▲ English immigrant George F. Whitworth helped to establish communities of faith in the Pacific Northwest, founding nearly twenty churches, including the First Presbyterian Church of Seattle. He also twice served as president of the University of Washington. Here are George and Mary Whitworth in about 1866. Daughters of the Pioneers of Washington State.

# Documents

Written records document much of our region's history.

The marriage certificate for the wedding of David Denny to Louisa Boren, uniting two of the Alki party families, is the first marriage certificate issued in King County. The handwritten document states, "This is to certify that David Denny & Louisa his wife was married by me a Justice of the Peace on the 23rd day of January AD 1853 at the house of A. A. Denny near the town of Seattle in King County Oregon Territory in the presence of A.A. Denny, wife & others. D.S. Maynard, J.P. [and] H.S. Yesler, Clerk."
◄ King County Archives.

Only a few months after David Denny and Louisa Boren were the first pioneer couple to be married in King County, Washington became a territory unto its own. By the time David J. Jones and Margaret M. Hutchinson of Newcastle were married in 1877, marriage certificates issued in King County had become considerably more elegant. Daughters of the Pioneers of Washington State. ▶

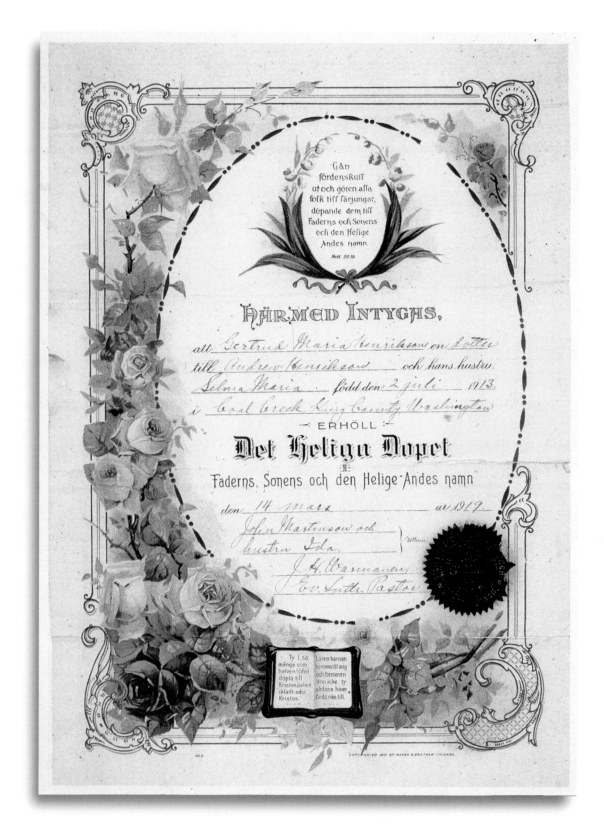

▲ Sacred documents also tell their own story of the lives of King County people. A beautiful baptismal certificate, translated from Swedish, records: "To Gertrude Maria Henrikson, Daughter of Andrew Henrikson and his wife Selma Maria, born on the second of July 1913, in Coal Creek, King County, Washington." Swede-Finn Historical Society.

▲ Between 1937 and 1940, a Works Progress Administration (WPA) project documented the existing structures of Seattle and King County for the King County Assessor's office. The unique collection offers the researcher a richly detailed record of the region during the Great Depression, on the eve of World War II. This property record card from 1940 includes a photo and information documenting the condition, value and ownership of a tavern in the town of Skykomish. Washington State Archives.

This Sammamish area cabin, built in 1888 by Swedish immigrants James and Johanna Isackson Bengston, is an excellent example of cabin construction. After James died, Johanna continued to live in the cabin until 1947. The cabin was located at what is now 3019-244th Avenue NE. Sammamish Heritage Society. ▶

# Country Settlers

◄ Nellie and Byron Kibler were the founding settlers of Enumclaw and their portrait dates to about 1900. Enumclaw Plateau Historical Society.

The portrait showing the Woodin family was done in about 1900; they were the first settlers in what is now Woodinville. Top row, left to right: Helen, Frank, and Mary Woodin, and lower row, Ira and Susan Woodin. The Woodin home housed the first post office, school and Sunday school, and was the stopping-over place for early river travelers. A whole town grew up around this family. Woodinville Historical Society. ►

# Japanese Settlers

▲ A 1915 photo shows a membership meeting of the Nihonjinkai (Japanese Community Club) held at Nippon Kan Hall. The members pose in front of the stage curtain that is richly painted with advertisements. Nippon Kan Hall was built in 1909, and quickly became a community center in Seattle's Nihonmachi, or Japantown. Seattle Buddhist Temple.

◄ Suzue and Masato Yamada posed for a portrait photograph after their wedding in 1922. The ceremony was held at the Thomas Buddhist Temple near Auburn. White River Valley Museum.

Here, Japanese families celebrate by making New Year's mochi, in 1915. The photo was taken on Meadowbrook Farm in the Upper Snoqualmie Valley. Mochi is a confection made from pounded, boiled sticky rice, and is a Japanese New Year's tradition. Snoqualmie Valley Historical Society. ▼

# Pioneer Artifacts

Settlers brought precious possessions west when they
settled in this far country. Some items reminded
them of home and family; others were essentials in
daily living, and others brought a touch of elegance
to cabins, farmhouses and city boarding houses.

This brass bell made its way to Washington Territory by way of the Oregon
Trail, and the family who owned it settled in West Seattle, on what is today
known as Beach Drive. Whenever a new family arrived, the neighbors
welcomed the newcomers by joining in a procession, led by a community
member ringing the bell. This bell also gaily rang in each New Year.
Southwest Seattle Historical Society. ▶

◀ The two piece suitcase (a kori) was
woven from willow whips, and was
used by Sen (Iwasaka) Maekawa when
she immigrated to the United States as
a picture bride in 1910. The number
and name were applied in 1942 when
the family was evacuated from Auburn
to wartime internment at the Pinedale
Detention Camp. White River Valley
Museum.

Sisters Elisabeth (Libbie) and Anna Peebles, two of Asa
Mercer's "girls," brought the trunk with them when
they arrived in Seattle, May 1866, aboard the steamer
*Continental*. These brave young women had traveled
from New York, taking a chance on the far Northwest.
Museum of History & Industry. ▶

▼ Whether to defend their wagons on the overland trek or to hunt deer in Puget Sound forests, settlers brought the best weapon they could when they settled in Washington Territory. A good example is this Whitney rifle, ca. 1850. Museum of History & Industry.

◄ When Charles and Ruth Jones migrated to Des Moines by way of the Panama Canal in 1919, they brought with them this three-branched candelabra. Des Moines Historical Society.

An early Norwegian immigrant carefully packed this spinning wheel, and carried it all the way from Norway to Seattle, in about 1910. Nordic Heritage Museum. ▼

◄ The doll was made by H.F. Beecher for Guendolen Carkeek, the only daughter in the family. Morgan Carkeek was a Cornish immigrant to Seattle, who initially made his living as a stonemason and eventually became very wealthy, building the post-fire Seattle of brick and stone. Born in 1892, Guendolen Carkeek began school in Seattle and later attended schools and convents in Europe. In 1929, she married a Russian Prince, Theodore Plestcheeff, whom she had met in Estonia. Museum of History & Industry.

The first settlers at Alki Point included young David Denny and Louisa Boren – the couple had traveled from Illinois together, fallen in love, and were soon married. Their 1853 land claim was north of the other settlers, running east to south Lake Union. Here Denny and his "Sweetbriar Bride" built first a cabin, and later a comfortable farmhouse where they raised their eight children. Here are paired oil portraits of the two. ▼

◄◄ Painting of Louisa Boren Denny. Museum of History & Industry.

◄ Painting of David Denny. Museum of History & Industry.

# What People Wore

◄ Local settlers paid attention to the ceremonies of life. Wealthy people had special costumes tailored to suit the event; others borrowed or sewed their own clothing. This wedding dress, worn by a happy bride in about 1900, is typical of thousands. Memory Lane Museum at Seattle Goodwill.

▲ The elegant boudoir gown was fashioned of burgundy and black velvet. It belonged to Margaret Tosh, daughter of early Redmond settler and farmer Adam Tosh. Eastside Heritage Center.

# The Changing Community

▲ Opportunities in the beauty industry were expanding in King County in the mid-20th century. These women were students at the Whiteside School of Cosmetology in 1945. Black Heritage Society of Washington State.

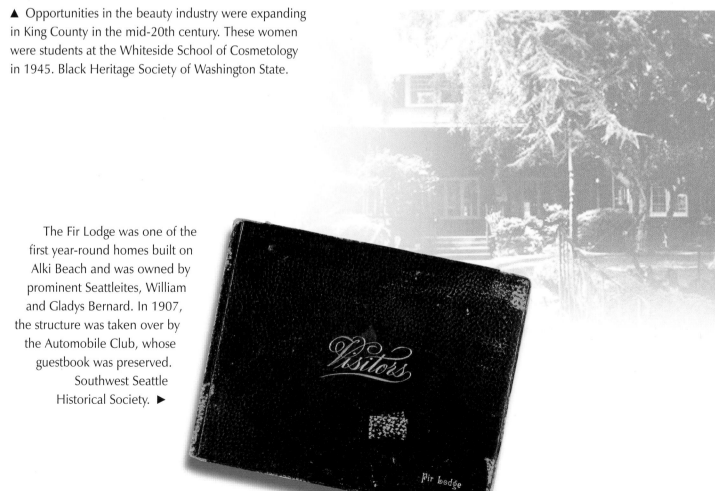

The Fir Lodge was one of the first year-round homes built on Alki Beach and was owned by prominent Seattleites, William and Gladys Bernard. In 1907, the structure was taken over by the Automobile Club, whose guestbook was preserved. Southwest Seattle Historical Society. ▶

# chapter three

## The Built Environment

*by Lawrence Kreisman*

Seattle and King County are just toddlers by European standards and brash adolescents compared to East Coast and Midwest neighbors. During the 17th and 18th centuries, when the thirteen colonies were bringing English and Continental lifestyles to America and clearing land for towns and cities, the Puget Sound area was a center for Native cultures, thriving with an abundance of natural resources, fish, game, land, navigable waterways, and a mild climate. Great longhouses were the first "mixed-use" buildings in the Northwest.

During the 19th century, the Industrial Revolution and the development of railroads pushed settlements westward to the goldfields of California and northward to Oregon Territory. But with the exception of Hudson's Bay Company trappers and early explorers, Puget Sound remained largely the province of Native American tribes because of its inaccessibility by overland routes.

The Federal Oregon Donation Land Act of 1850 did much to encourage settlement, particularly along waterways that were accessible by boat or canoe. In 1850, John Holgate navigated the Duwamish River to Elliott Bay. In 1851, Luther Collins, Henry Van Asselt, Jacob Maple, Samuel Maple, and their families settled along the Duwamish, followed by others who farmed the White River valley. The first Euro-

▲ One of the earliest depictions of Seattle's burgeoning cityscape, the 1869 panorama demonstrates the vision of Seattle pioneers as they endeavored to improve the land and create a livable city. Washington State Historical Society.

▲ This ca. 1920 painting by Fokko Tadama depicts the White-Henry-Stuart Building under construction at 4th Avenue and University Street. As Seattle was building, so were the outlying areas of King County. Lured by the promise of cheap land, space and opportunity, people found reasons to build their lives in a variety of communities outside of Seattle. Museum of History & Industry.

American settlers in "New York Alki"—the Denny, Terry, Boren, and Bell families—traveled overland to Oregon and sailed north to reach the shores of the Sound in 1851. They moved to a more protected location the following spring, naming it Seattle after a tribal chief. Henry Yesler's steam-powered lumber mill became the lifeblood of the new community.

Seattle's first real spurt of growth resulted from the construction of several important rail lines that formed vital links to lumber, farming, and coal mining communities in western King County. The influx of settlers from the East and Midwest stimulated a thriving business center in Seattle, nearly all of it constructed from the local material of choice—wood. An 1889 fire destroyed the central business district. Fortunately, the fire occurred at a time of prosperity, and businessmen immediately rebuilt the commercial core in brick, stone, cast iron, and heavy timber. Architects from the East, the Midwest, and California flocked to Seattle to take advantage of the building opportunities.

The discovery of gold in the Yukon in 1897 prompted a second and greater influx of people to the shores of Puget Sound. Seattle became the major banking, outfitting, and departure point for Alaska and, subsequently, the settling place for many of those returning from the goldfields. Rail and interurban lines opened up tracts of land for development of homes and businesses. Real estate promotional materials encouraged newcomers to invest in property along Madison Street leading to Lake Washington, or further afield, such as Columbia City, Riverton, or Magnolia. Tourist hotels, such as the short-lived C.C. Calkins Hotel on Mercer Island, found a following in the city and the county.

This newel-post staircase can be found in the Neely Mansion. Neely Mansion Association. ▼

▲ Pioneer Aaron Neely sat for this portrait ca. 1900. Greater Kent Historical Society.

▲ The Neely Mansion, a unique Victorian farmhouse, was constructed in 1874 by early American settler Aaron Neely in the Green River Valley. Located near a ferry crossing, it became a social center for the valley. After its tenure as the Neely home, the elegant farmhouse was leased to a succession of immigrant newcomers: Swiss dairy farmers, Japanese dairy farmers and Filipino vegetable-and-berry farmers. Since its restoration, the Neely Mansion has been listed on the National Register for Historic Places, but it also is a landmark to the changing peoples of King County. Neely Mansion Association.

▲ This is a detail from the Neely Mansion bathhouse. The Neelys lived in the Mansion only a few years, finding it somewhat isolated, and moved back to Auburn. Swiss, Japanese and Filipino tenant farmers occupied the property over the next several decades; one of the families built a Japanese-style bathhouse in the 1930s. Neely Mansion Association.

The agricultural wealth of King County was reflected in such substantial homesteads as that of the Neely family in Auburn and the Dougherty family in Duvall. Immigrants from Europe and Asia brought their familiarity with building types and styles to the region. Brick single-room occupancy hotels and commercial buildings in Seattle's Chinatown sported family-association meeting rooms with elaborate balconies. Scandinavians built meeting halls modeled after Norwegian stave churches and Finnish saunas like the one in the collection of the Nordic Heritage Museum.

The city's heightened prosperity during the second decade of the 20th century was evidenced in brick- and terracotta-faced skyscrapers, banking headquarters, and department stores that arose north of the older business district.

As if to announce to the world that Seattle had come of age, the city staged the Alaska-Yukon-Pacific Exposition in 1909 that promoted Seattle as the commercial "Gateway to Alaska and the Orient." The national City Beautiful ideal played out in a commercial and retail district on the original university grounds developed by the Metropolitan Building Company beginning in 1907 and depicted in an oil painting by Fokko Tadama, a Dutch immigrant, showing the White Henry Stuart Building under construction on 4th Avenue.

But it was as the City Practical that Seattle showed its muscle. J. D. Ross developed City Light and committed the city to improved utilities. Largely because of the leadership of two engineers, R. H. Thomson and George Cotterill, the city established an effective water and sewer system. Engineering feats on a scale seldom attempted in an American city produced extensive regrading (raising and lowering of streets using hydraulic hoses and excavating equipment), filling of tide flats, and cutting of canals to provide shipping lanes

The Calkins Hotel was built in 1891 on Mercer Island when the only access was by boat. Mercer Island Historical Society. ▼

▲ A wood-stove door plate from the Dougherty House. Duvall Historical Society.

▲ The Dougherty House is an historical farmstead located on Northeast Cherry Valley Road, Duvall. The wooden frame house, built in 1888, has been restored. The farmhouse, outbuildings and barn are some of the oldest standing structures in the Snoqualmie River valley. The farmstead was designated an historic site in 1983. Duvall Historical Society.

◄ The interior of the Dougherty House might have appeared like this in 1888. The bedside table and chamber pot, as well as blacksmith tools and the interiors of the Dougherty House buildings, typify the lifestyle of many Duvall citizens in the late 1800s. Duvall Historical Society.

◄ This Finnish sauna was built ca. 1900. The sauna is preserved as a final structure from what was once a thriving Finnish community on Finn Hill, northeast of Lake Washington. Nordic Heritage Museum.

and building sites for the expanding city. In the process, the water level of Lake Washington was lowered, adding significantly to shoreline parks and boulevards proposed by the Olmsted Brothers.

Regrading and fill projects lasted into the 1930s, increasing access to developing residential districts to the north and east of the downtown. Typically, realtors promoted these areas, such as Kenmore and Shoreline, with colorful prose. The opening of the Lacey V. Murrow Bridge across Lake Washington in 1940 stimulated residential growth on Mercer Island and the Eastside. The post–World War II shortage of housing spurred developments in expanding suburban areas outside Seattle city limits and the annexation by the city of suburban areas. The postwar "baby boom," job opportunities, a freeway system and a second bridge across Lake Washington in the 1960s led to further dramatic changes in King County that shifted it from rural to suburban and urban. Roadside architecture became a fixture of these communities— burger huts and drive-ins as eateries but also as gathering places for the younger generation.

By the early 1970s, new interests in historic preservation, adaptive reuse of older buildings, revitalization of old neighborhoods, and the creation of new environments for living in downtown resulted in the establishment of Seattle historic districts. In 1973, a Landmarks Preservation Ordinance set the stage for nominating and designating individual landmarks. With a similar mindset, concerned citizens and King County officials encouraged the county to undertake an inventory and evaluation of significant historic sites beginning in 1972. The county established an Office of Historic Preservation in 1978 and adopted a Landmarks Ordinance in 1980.

In 1974, the Historic Seattle Preservation and Development Authority was established to do meaningful preservation projects. One of

▲ The Curtis family members were founding settlers of Houghton, in the Kirkland area. This photo of the Curtis family in 1890 shows James and Will Curtis working on the homestead with young Wilbur Curtis driving the horse. Kirkland Heritage Society.

The sign advertised lots for sale at Columbia View. Real estate was the original industry in Columbia City. The town was created by developers after the streetcar line went through in 1890. People were lured from downtown Seattle by easy terms of $300, $10 down and a dollar a week without interest: the idea of "pioneering" with the convenience of street cars. Rainier Valley Historical Society. ▶

the largest was the restoration and adaptive reuse of the House of the Good Shepherd into space for non-profit offices, schools and a senior center. The restoration of its chapel into a first-class concert venue was completed in 2008, in time for the building's centennial.

Seattle and King County government, public-development authorities, and non-profit organizations such as museums and historical societies have protected a significant number of visual reminders of built history and have acted as catalysts to encourage the restoration, rehabilitation and reuse of built resources. They share that burden and its many successes with the efforts of individual property owners who have pride in their businesses, homes, gardens, and farmlands. They are truly the major contributors to preserving the built legacy of King County.

*Lawrence Kreisman, Hon. AIA Seattle, is Program Director of Historic Seattle. He has been recognized for bringing public attention to the Northwest's architectural heritage and its preservation through courses, tours, exhibits, lectures, articles and books, and program development. His publications include* Apartments by Anhald; The Stimson Legacy: Architecture in the Urban West; The Bloedel Reserve: Gardens in the Forest; Made to Last: Historic Preservation in Seattle and King County; *and* The Arts and Crafts Movement in the Pacific Northwest *(with Glenn Mason), as well as design features in* Pacific Northwest, *the Sunday magazine of* The Seattle Times.

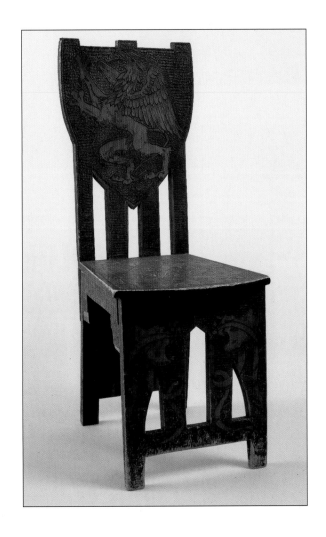

Panoramic View of Riverton from South Riverton Heights, Showing Elevation Along River

▲ View of Riverton from a real estate brochure, 1907. Tukwila Historical Society.

◄ View of downtown Seattle looking east on Madison Street from Second Avenue, 1909. Washington State Historical Society.

◄ Typifying Norwegian furniture styles of the late 19th century, this chair was made by a Norwegian immigrant to Seattle, ca. 1900. Nordic Heritage Museum.

◄ This chest of drawers (viewed from the back) was made from explosives boxes. Renton History Museum.

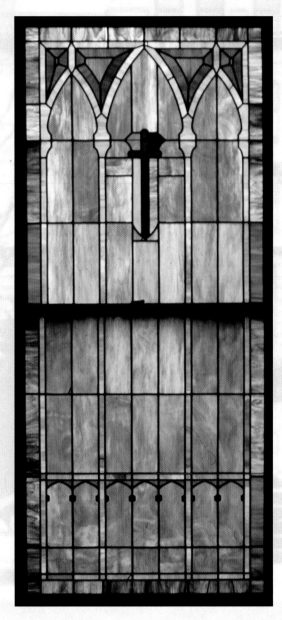

Detail of stained glass inside the Home of the Good Shepherd. Historic Seattle. ►

◄ Photo of interior of the Home of the Good Shepherd, built in 1907. Historic Seattle.

◄ Detail of door inside the Home of the Good Shepherd. Historic Seattle.

Proclaiming Seattle as the "Gateway to Alaska and the Orient," a 1913 advertisement shows the brand-new Smith Tower's prominence on the Seattle waterfront. For many years, it was famous as the tallest building west of the Mississippi. Washington State Historical Society. ▶

(Opposite, top) Named for the view of Lake Washington that could be seen from many of the lots in the development, Lago Vista in northwest King County prominently advertises property for sale at the real estate office on 15th Avenue NE and NE 192nd Street in 1928. Shoreline Historical Museum.

(Opposite, bottom) Once located at 63rd and Bothell Way, Kenmore Realty's signage in 1934 advertised "Large View Lots on this Hill with Water and Lights for $200." Kenmore Heritage Society.

SEATTLE

THE GATEWAY TO ALASKA and the ORIENT

The car culture brought another wave of development for areas outside the big city – more roads, more houses, and a different kind of built environment. "Drive-ins" became the new business genre, and "fast" was the new watchword. Establishments such as Triple XXX Root Beer and Whizburger became known as fast-food joints.

A syrup container from a Triple XXX Drive-in, ca. 1941. Renton History Museum. ▶

"Whizburger" sandwich shop sign. Highline Historical Society. ▼

# chapter four

# Making a Living

*by Mary T. Henry*

From the fish-filled waters of Puget Sound to the shrouded hills of evergreen trees, the land that became King County was a beacon to early settlers who farmed, fished, mined and logged there. Native Americans were already there, thriving on bounties of the land and water which housed, clothed, and fed them. Later, as people from Europe and Asia came to this area of rich natural resources, they labored and contributed to its economic vitality in unique ways.

The first settlers, Luther Collins, Henry Van Asselt and Joseph Maple looked upon the Duwamish River Valley as rich agricultural land and began farming there in 1851. Hop growing in the late 1880s became the center of the economy in the valley and later supported the world's sixth-largest output of beer. Japanese farmers found the soil there, in the White River Valley and east of Lake Washington, ideal for growing berries. By 1920, they supplied more than 70 percent of the fruit and vegetables for Western Washington. Dairy farming flourished and the Danes introduced the first cooperative in the Pacific Northwest.

Logging became a vibrant industry after the first shipment of shingles from Alki in 1851 and when Henry Yesler introduced his steam-powered sawmill in 1852. Scandinavian immigrants soon occupied most of the logging camps in the late 1800s due to overpopulation, famine and unemployment in Norway, Sweden and Finland. They were then, and continue to be, leaders in the fishing industry. Commercial canneries were staffed by low-paid Chinese and Filipino workers.

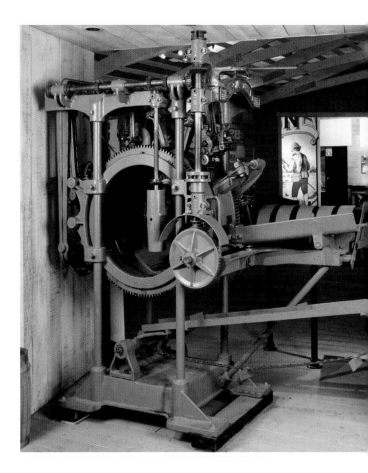

▲ This salmon-butchering machine, patented as the "Iron Chink," was named for the Chinese laborers it was invented to replace. Although much of the salmon-canning process was mechanized in the early years of the 20th century, the butchering process was done by hand by laborers who migrated up and down the North Pacific Coast every year. The machine could perform the work of 50 butchers. It was displayed at the 1909 Alaska-Yukon-Pacific Exposition. Museum of History & Industry.

▲ Detail of salmon-butchering machine patented as "Iron Chink." Museum of History & Industry.

These medical instruments were owned by Dr. David S. Maynard, who arrived in Seattle in 1852. His original plans to salt salmon for the San Francisco market failed, but he set up Seattle's first store, selling medicine and general merchandise in his salting works on First Avenue and Main Street. It was "Doc" Maynard who first proposed naming the new city Seattle after the chief of the local Native American people. Maynard also served as Seattle's Justice of the Peace. Museum of History & Industry.

▲ A letter dated May 3, 1853, from John and Sarah Denny to his mother, describes Henry Yesler's Mill and the conditions in Seattle. Washington State Historical Society.

By 1878 coal outpaced the lumber industry after Chinese laborers, who also dug the canal between Lake Union and Salmon Bay, extended the Seattle and Walla Walla Railroad to Newcastle, allowing coal to be hauled to Elliott Bay piers. Mines in Ravensdale, Newcastle, Renton and Franklin were worked by a variety of ethnic laborers including African American, Welsh, Italian, German, Lithuanian, Serbian, Polish, Chinese and Russian.

As would be expected, laborers in the early economy began to organize because of poor working conditions, poor pay and long hours. By 1900 there were 40 labor unions in Seattle alone. In addition to the United Mine Workers union and the longshoremen's union, waitresses, tanners, cigar makers, brewers, barbers, shingle weavers, retail clerks and others were organizing for better working conditions.

Women labored in fisheries, canneries, laundries, breweries, hotels, restaurants, bawdy houses and confectioneries. Many worked 14-hour days, seven days a week. By 1911, Washington State had become one of the first states in the nation to grant women an eight-hour workday and also to insure injured workers. In 1919, Seattle was paralyzed for five days because of a general strike, the first to be held in the country.

Professionals and other support groups arrived in proportion to the population. Physicians and dentists, lawyers, health-care workers, and educators all worked to enhance the quality of life for the residents of King County.

Perhaps because of its pioneering history or its location on the outer edge of the country, King County also has proven to be a fertile area for entrepreneurs.

William Boeing and Bill Gates are the respective founders of a world-renowned

Indian Basket Sellers
Seattle

▲ This postcard, titled "Indian Basket Sellers/ Seattle," depicts Native street vendors in Seattle with "Frederick & Nelson, Womens Costumes, Suits, Furs Etc." as background. The card was published by "the writing room of Frederick & Nelson, Seattle" and postmarked in 1912. University of Washington Libraries.

◄ This photo of a small logging engine at Woodinville Lumber Co. represents a change in the transport of lumber. Small steam trains replaced the horse and oxen; trains took less time and could carry more product out of the woods. Woodinville Historical Society.

▲ This log cart, drawn by oxen, was photographed in 1885. The Bothell Brothers Tramway was a crude track of six-inch-diameter pole rails, on which cars ran on concave wheels. The tramway was laid west of First Street to the Sammamish River. After 1917, logs were floated to the mills by way of the new Montlake Cut. Bothell Historical Museum Society.

aerospace company and the software giant Microsoft, but there are other examples of locally founded industries that have achieved national or global recognition. The area's first brewery, which became Rainier, was launched by John Claussen and Edward Sweeny in 1883 and became the fifth-largest brewery in the world. On Vashon Island, Masahiro Mukai pioneered strawberry farming by introducing new methods of freezing berries for sale nationwide and overseas. Eddie Bauer launched a mail order firm dealing in cold weather clothing; the Nordstrom family developed a clothing store with branches in major cities around the country; Jeff Bezos founded the online company Amazon.com; and biotech companies sprout throughout the county.

King County's museums and historical societies have garnered photographs, documents and artifacts which witness how its citizens have labored, created, and innovated through one and a half centuries.

---

*Mary T. Henry is a retired Seattle Public School librarian and author of* Tribute: Seattle Public Places Named for Black People, *for which she received an AKCHO Award.*

*She was the editor of the* Black Heritage Society Newsletter *from 1993 until 2003 and has been a writer for Blackpast.org. She has been a staff writer for HistoryLink.org since its inception in 1998. She is also the archivist for Epiphany Parish in Seattle and has served on the boards of the Seattle Education Foundation, Association of King County Historical Organizations and Seattle's Landmarks Preservation Board.*

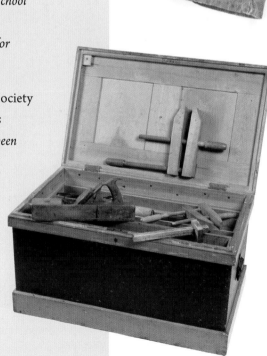

▲ The outfit known as a "Tin Suit" was rubbed with paraffin wax for waterproofing. It was worn by loggers at John Nelson Logging in Cedar River area, ca. 1925. Eastside Heritage Center.

◄ This tool chest and tools belonged to Danish immigrant Julius Christianson. Museum of History & Industry.

▲ This Columbia mill was photographed in 1891. These giant logs
built Columbia City and helped to rebuild Seattle after the 1889 fire.
Rainier Valley Historical Society.

▲ This Rayonier #24 Logging Speeder, 1951, was built by Gibson
Manufacturing of Seattle. The 65-man speeder was designed to transport
loggers to the cutting sites. Northwest Railway Museum.

Dory used by Norwegian fisherman.
Nordic Heritage Museum.

This fishing boat is the salmon seiner *Lilly*. Puget Sound Maritime Historical Society.

◄ Lumber was the earliest driving force behind the King County economy. Wood was shipped to ports in California, Mexico, South America, and across the Pacific. This photo shows the schooner *Wawona* loaded with lumber in 1899. *Wawona* was typical of the lumber schooners that loaded wood from King County sawmills, especially at Seattle's deep-water port on Elliott Bay. A schooner like the *Wawona* could sail with a crew of eight (Captain, First Mate, Second Mate, Cook, and four seamen), unlike a square-rigger which needed a much larger crew to climb the masts. Lumber schooners needed no fuel but the wind to compete with steamboats. Northwest Seaport.

▲ Chinese sailors/workmen take a break on a freighter. Puget Sound Maritime Historical Society.

Hops Basket, ca. 1890. A seasonal activity, hops picking gave some Native American families and others an opportunity to participate in the cash economy. The hops blight that began in 1892 took its toll on many crops around Puget Sound. Later, the 1920 prohibition of alcohol would take its toll as well. Eastside Heritage Center. ▶

▲ Photograph by Asahel Curtis of the Marine Employees Union, labeled December 28, 1922. Washington State Historical Society.

Property of Museum of History & Industry, Seattle

◄ This photo shows the fireboat *Duwamish* fighting the Grand Trunk fire in 1914. Although the Grand Trunk Pacific Dock was destroyed, fireboats *Duwamish* and *Snoqualmie* were able to prevent the fire from jumping to the steamship-passenger and freight terminal at Colman Dock, shown in the right background. The new Smith Tower is in the left background. Colman Dock has since been replaced with a modern ferry terminal, and the fireboat *Duwamish* is a National Historic Landmark, moored at the Historic Ships Wharf at Lake Union Park. Museum of History & Industry.

The postcard by Darius Kinsey is titled "Siwash and two Klootchmen Hop Picking in Snoqualmie Hop Fields." Snoqualmie Valley Historical Society. ▶

Photo of woman with hops. Des Moines Historical Society. ▶

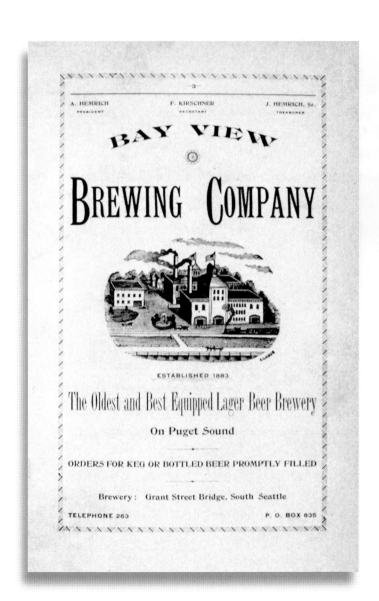

◄ Directory for the City of Seattle with advertisement for Bay View Brewing Company, 1892. University of Washington Libraries.

Workers harvest hops in White River Valley, ca. 1880. Hops were grown near Titusville, now Kent, from 1880 to 1889. Greater Kent Historical Society. ▼

▲ Milking stool used at Avondale Farm in Redmond, ca. 1910. Eastside Heritage Center.

▲ This Bellevue Vegetable Growers Association label touts Belle-View Brand Washington Peas. Eastside Heritage Center.

▲ Built in 1881, the Carnation Creamery was originally constructed as a hotel by speculators hoping that a racetrack would be built in Kent. After being vacant for nearly eight years, it was converted into the Pacific Coast Condensed Milk Company in 1889. The building later became Kent Hardware and is now known as the Creamery block. Greater Kent Historical Society.

▲ The Kelfner Fruit and Vegetable Stand was located at 112th SE and Bellevue Way. John and Frances Kelfner came to Bellevue in 1911. Eastside Heritage Center.

This incubator held 60 eggs. The advent of "electric farming" gave chicken ranches a boost in production. Eastside Heritage Center. ▶

# Merchants

Mrs. McDonald opened this general store in 1891 and sold it the same year to William D. Gibbon. The building was turned into a creamery in 1894 and became a restaurant in 1906. That same year, the Gibbon house at right was moved to the left of the store and turned into a hotel to make room for the Milwaukee Railroad right-of-way. Maple Valley Historical Society. ▶

Early Jewish settlers in Western Washington often made their living as peddlers and merchants. Cooper and Levy Pioneer Outfitters, shown here not long after the beginning of the Klondike Gold Rush, outfitted would-be miners with everything from blankets to gold pans, dried apples, and tools. Washington State Jewish Historical Society. ▼

◄ In a rare interior photo, ca. 1900, the North Bend general store's stock is well documented: fresh produce, socks hanging behind the counter, brooms hanging from the ceiling, a coffee grinder and richly stocked ornate glass cases invite customers to browse and buy the store's fine merchandise. Snoqualmie Valley Historical Society.

The William Hannan house, now the Bothell Museum, contains many artifacts belonging to the well-known Bothell businessman. The ca. 1900 plate displayed on the plate rail in the home's dining room is one of the premiums that Hannan gave to special customers. Bothell Historical Museum Society. ▶

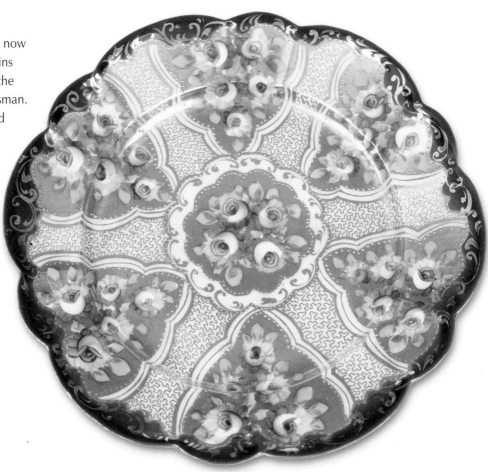

◀ A 1937 advertisement for Barney O'Connor's Drug Stores listing locations at the Olympic Hotel, Sorrento Hotel and Fifth Avenue Drug Company also acknowledges the importance of the company's Japanese-speaking customers. Washington State Historical Society.

**BARNEY O'CONNOR'S DRUG STORES**

| Olympic Hotel Pharmacy 4th & University EL. 3570 | Sorrento Pharmacy Terry & Madison Ma. 0444 | 5th Avenue Drug Company Fifth & Union Ma. 1232 |

*Barney O'Connor Proprietor*

本行特聘實驗製藥師專接配
藥單兼售各種花粉香品價廉
物美久已爲華友所知如蒙惠
顧請由電話向零四四四號即
MA.0444通知本行即送
至貴處送貨免費華友光顧特
表歡迎
柯很那藥行主人謹啟

65

The Seattle Bon Marché was opened by Edward Nordhoff in 1890, one year after Seattle's Great Fire. It became a standard by which other such stores were measured, and its name was applied to a variety of merchandise, such as a 1909 fine china **Alaska-Yukon-Pacific Exposition** souvenir plate, with a stamp clearly identifying both the maker and the seller. Klondike Gold Rush Museum. ▼

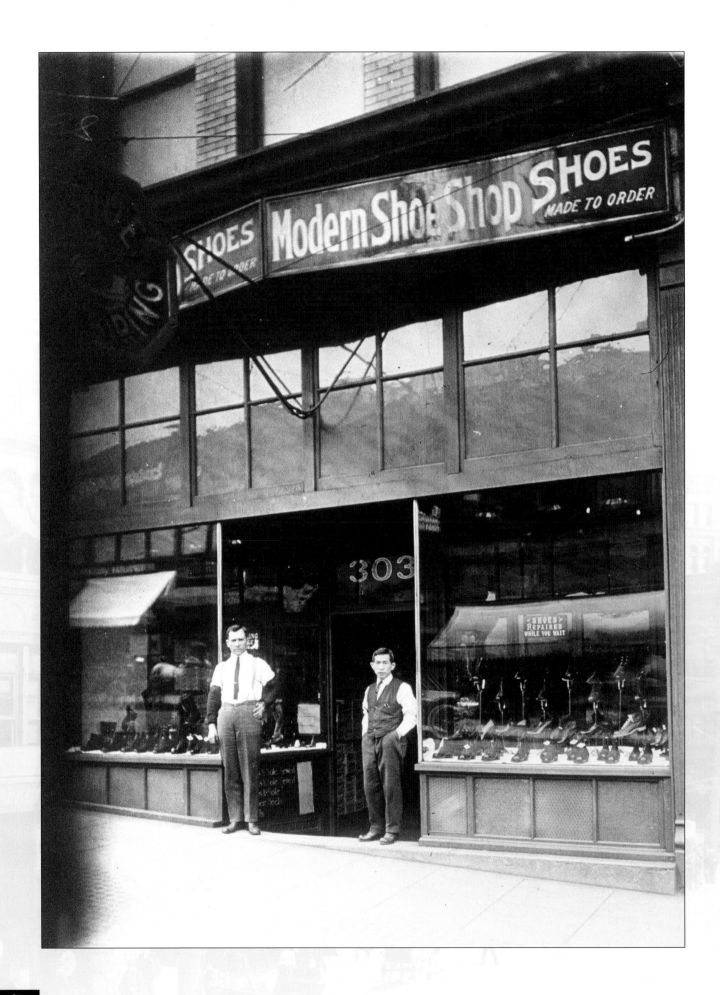

◄ The Modern Shoe Shop, where shoes could be made to order, was owned by proprietor T. Makino, shown here on the right, in front of his business, ca. 1910. The shop was located at 303 S Main in Seattle's International District. Wing Luke Asian Museum.

▲ Solomon "Sam" Calvo is the mustachioed proprietor standing in front of the Sephardic Waterfront Fish Market and Oyster Company, ca. 1918, at the Pike Place Market in Seattle. Washington State Jewish Historical Society.

# chapter five

# Transportation

*by Alan Stein*

An examination of King County's modern transportation corridors reveals routes laid out centuries ago. Native American villages and encampments tended to be near water for ease of travel by canoe. Farther inland, trails crossed over valleys and hillsides. Mountain passes extended trade and communication east of the Cascades.

When King County's first white settlers arrived in 1851, they took up residence on the shores of Elliott Bay and along the Duwamish River. Established trails served them well, but once land claims were made in what would become downtown Seattle, the county's first street grid was platted to better accommodate horses and wagons. Docks and piers were built along Seattle's waterfront for the growing numbers of boats and ships on Puget Sound.

As the village grew to become the county's main port of call, goods traveled to and from outlying communities along routes that had been in use for ages. Travel to the fertile White River Valley was accomplished by boat, or along Indian trails. These trails grew into roads. Similar travel patterns expanded on or around Lake Washington, Lake Sammamish, the Sammamish River and the Cedar River.

The discovery of coal in the mountains and foothills led to rail lines that often paralleled rivers and streams. Meanwhile, larger rail lines from back east crossed mountain passes and connected King County with the rest of the nation. By this time, a vast "Mosquito Fleet" of passenger ferries connected all major communities along Puget Sound.

▲ The *Fortuna*, shown on Lake Washington in 1909, was built at the Anderson shipyard in Houghton. It was used on the lake as an excursion steamer during the Alaska-Yukon-Pacific Exposition. The steamer later became part of the ferry system serving Lake Washington. Kirkland Heritage Society.

# By Water

◄ An integral part of Salish Indian culture, the Western Red Cedar dugout hunting canoe is typical of those constructed by John Cheshlahud of the Duwamish Tribe at his house on Portage Bay. There is room for one or two paddlers and some gear in this ca. 1880 example. Found on the Tacoma Narrows in 1912, it was donated by Lloyd Reed in 1983, after 70 years of use as a family boat. The Center for Wooden Boats.

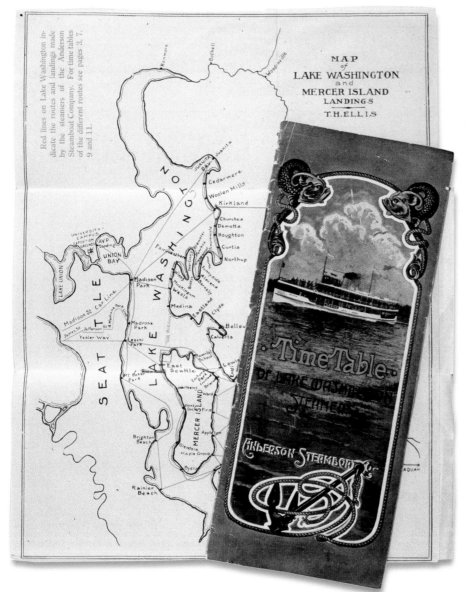

◄ This time table, issued by Anderson Steamboat Company, and the route map by T.H. Ellis indicate Alaska-Yukon-Pacific Exposition routes and landings for Lake Washington and Mercer Island ferries. Washington State Historical Society.

By 1900, most towns and villages in King County had their own street grids. Seattle overlaid its grid with streetcars, while interurban trains soon made their way north and south to Everett and Tacoma, making stops in smaller cities along the way. But this foray into light rail was relatively short-lived, as commuters and travelers embraced a new form of transportation – the automobile.

King County's first motor car arrived in 1900, but automobile use didn't become widespread until the 1910s, following the introduction of Henry Ford's mass-produced Model T. As more and more people drove autos, interurban and streetcar use fell off. Interurban service to Tacoma ended in 1928 with the opening of Highway 99, and service to Everett ended 11 years later.

The auto age brought more changes to the county's transportation corridors. Narrow roads which were once trails had to be expanded. In some cases, geography trumped history and new routes were plotted when expansion proved unwieldy.

Even the old canoe routes were overtaken by automobiles. Beginning in the 1910s, auto ferries were the preferred form of travel on Lake Washington. By the 1950s, rapid growth on the Eastside necessitated a quicker route, and the first floating bridge brought ferry service across the lake to an end.

In 1956, President Eisenhower signed the National Defense Highways Act, unleashing federal funds for an interstate highway system. Within a few years I-5 cleaved the western side of King County from top to bottom, while I-90 passed through the county's midsection from mountains to sound. Cloverleafs, offramps, and onramps provided connections to each city along the wide concrete and asphalt paths. Some joked that the county would be completely paved over by century's end.

▲ A 1901 Seattle Shipping Agency poster advertises a steamship trip in four days from Seattle to Valdez and the Copper River on the *Oregon*; George Seeley, Master. Washington State Historical Society.

◄ The *City of Bothell* passenger steamboat, shown here in about 1910, was used on the Sammamish River. It linked Lake Sammamish to Lake Washington before the Lake Washington Ship Canal and Hiram M. Chittenden Locks opened in 1916, which caused the lowering of the lakes. Bothell Historical Museum Society.

▲ The 1922 *SS Virginia V* was built for the West Pass Transportation Company to carry cargo and passengers from Vashon Island to Seattle and Tacoma. It is the last surviving boat from the "The Mosquito Fleet," a large group of privately owned ferries that served all of Puget Sound and Lake Washington. Puget Sound Maritime Historical Society.

◄ A number of boats belonging to Puget Sound's "The fleet" are seen at Colman Dock, in Elliott Bay. The Mosquito Fleet included dozens of small, privately owned steamers that carried freight and passengers in the late 19th and early 20th centuries. Puget Sound Maritime Historical Society.

But as highways quickly filled with cars, local voters sought ways to ease the traffic burden. Bus service increased, and in 1988 a two-thirds majority endorsed accelerated planning for rail service. In 2000, the first Sound Transit "Sounder" commuter trains rolled between Seattle and Tacoma almost a century after interurban cars linked the two cities.

Work continues on light rail, and streetcars have once again taken to the streets. And although the highways are still filled with cars, commuters continue to seek out ways to ease their travels, either through carpooling, telecommuting, bicycling, bus service, or by moving closer to their places of work.

Modern travelers may have more modes of travel than did Washington's first citizens, but the paths they choose are quite well-worn.

*Alan Stein is an author and staff historian at* HistoryLink.org, *the online encyclopedia for Washington state history. Alan is also past president of the Association of King County Historical Organizations.*

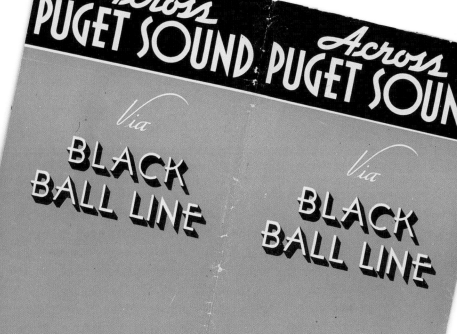

◀ Photographed by Asahel Curtis in 1935 shortly after the *Kalakala's* inaugural launch, the snackbar of the much-celebrated art deco ferry was noteworthy for its grand style. The *Kalakala* ran primarily between Seattle and Bremerton until 1962. Washington State Historical Society.

◀ The life preserver from the *Kalakala* is one of many rescued artifacts from the art deco ferry. Kalakala Foundation.

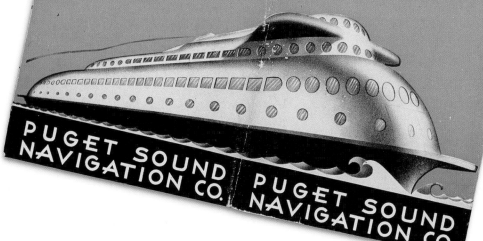

▲ The 1935 *Kalakala* time table documents the operating company, Puget Sound Navigation Company, and its Black Ball Line. Kalakala Foundation.

# By Railroad

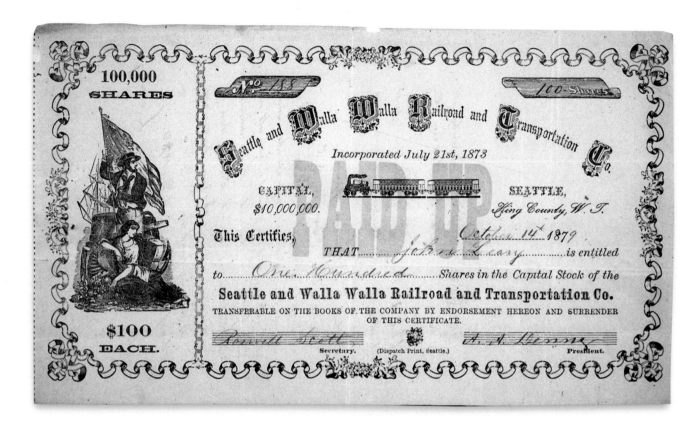

▲ This stock certificate for the Seattle and Walla Walla Railroad was issued in 1878. After the Northern Pacific Railway chose Tacoma as the West Coast terminus for the transcontinental line in 1873, Seattle boosters responded by organizing a drive to build the Seattle and Walla Walla Railroad. This line was intended to run from Seattle to connect with the Northern Pacific at Walla Walla. The trustees, including Arthur Denny, J.M. Colman and Dexter Horton, sold stock in the company, issuing certificates. Construction on the Seattle and Walla Walla Railroad began in the spring of 1874 at Georgetown, south of Seattle, reaching Renton in 1877. Chinese laborers, organized by Chin Gee Hee, extended the line as far as Newcastle in 1878, connecting the coal country of south King County to the coal bunkers at Pike Street on Elliott Bay. In 1880, the Oregon Improvement Company purchased the Seattle and Walla Walla, then renamed the Columbia and Puget Sound Railroad. In 1951, it was merged into the Great Northern Railway. Washington State Historical Society.

◄ The Seattle, Lake Shore and Eastern Railroad depot in what is now Issaquah was constructed in 1889. A modern-day photo shows how the depot has been restored to look as it once did when passengers on SLS&E arrived at what was the heart of Gilman. Issaquah Historical Society.

The Seattle, Lake Shore, and Eastern Railroad Company, begun in 1885, was backed by both local and East Coast funding. The first division of the SLS&E was built from Seattle along the western shore of Lake Washington and then east to Gilman – now Issaquah – with a focus on bringing coal into Seattle and to the coal bunkers at Elliott Bay. Service to Gilman began in 1888. The railroad was eventually purchased by the Northern Pacific. The map confirms the earliest stations, and consequently early settlement patterns brought about by the railroad. Northwest Railway Museum. ►

▲ The covered bridge on Renton Road was built in 1903 by the Union Pacific Railroad to carry traffic over its tracks. It was known by several names: Allentown Covered Bridge, Foster Covered Bridge, and Steele Hill Bridge. Sparks spewing from the smokestacks of the steam locomotives passing below caught the bridge on fire a number of times. Tukwila Historical Society.

▲ A woman returns from Seattle to the Tukwila Interurban Station at the bottom of Tukwila Hill, 1904. Just two years before, the Puget Sound Traction, Light & Power Company had completed the line from Seattle to Tacoma, calling it the Puget Sound Electric Railway. Tukwila Historical Society.

◄ A 1950 photo shows Auburn's Northern Pacific roundhouse and turntable, built in 1913. The rail yard generated local employment and a boost in population for the town. White River Valley Museum.

▲ This photograph of a Northern Pacific Railway Company train at the King Street Station, ca. 1910, was taken by A.M. Deig. University of Washington Libraries Special Collections Division.

# By Streetcar

Unlike the relatively quick construction of the southern division of the Interurban from Seattle to Tacoma, which was completed in about two years, the rail line north of Seattle took ten years to reach Everett. The Interurban was a major factor in the early development of the north-south corridor, and today's Shoreline area owes much of its current arrangement to that first method of rapid transit. Shown is a northward view of the Ronald Station, at 175th and Aurora, in 1910. The station was named after Judge T. Ronald, King County Superior Court Judge from 1909 to 1949, and Mayor of Seattle in 1892 and 1893. Shoreline Historical Museum. ▼

◄ Streetcars were not without their dangers, as illustrated by this Rainier Valley wreck at Willow Street in 1910. A runaway rail car carrying coal from Newcastle collided with the passenger streetcar, killing one and injuring numerous others. Rainier Valley Historical Society.

▲ Louis Hipkins - "Pa Hip" - poses at the window of one of the "Hipkins work cars" that he designed and built. Well known for his shop-built cars, Hipkins was a repairman on the streetcar line for 47 years. Rainier Valley Historical Society.

▲ Seen here in 1936 as streetcars pass over, the Fremont Bridge reconnected the neighborhoods that had been severed by the construction of the Ship Canal which opened in 1916. The bridge was completed in 1917, and is listed on the National Register for Historic Places. Seattle Municipal Archives.

▲ A Seattle Municipal Railway ticket from January 1940 shows the rules and variety of options for the rider. Seattle Municipal Archives.

This 1907 sign, now restored, marked the last stop on the Fauntleroy streetcar line. It became known as "Endolyne" because the conductor, W. C. Fonda, would call out "end o' line!" when the car approached the turn-around where a group of small beach cottages could be accessed. Southwest Seattle Historical Society. ▼

▲ Endolyne station ca. 1934. Seattle Municipal Archives.

## By Road

Seattleites have their photo taken on a drive to Riverton Heights, between Burien and Tukwila, for a picnic, ca. 1915. Highline Historical Society. ▶

A 1907 touring car is caught in mid-breakdown. Such problems were frequent occurrences for early autos, adding to the trials and tribulations of pioneering motorists. Washington State Historical Society. ▶

The construction of Ambaum Boulevard, which connected Burien and White Center to Seattle, was facilitated by this early steam-powered ditch-digging machine, ca. 1923. Highline Historical Society.

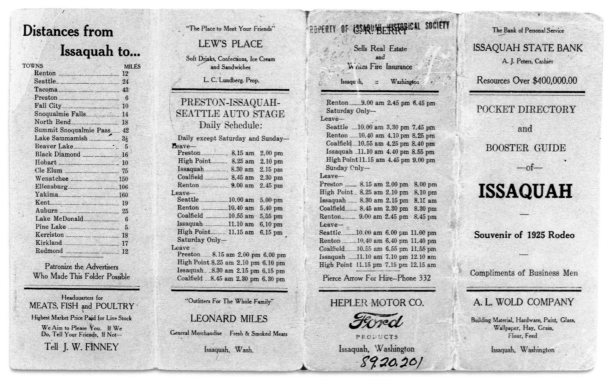

**Distances from Issaquah to...**

| TOWNS | MILES |
|---|---|
| Renton | 12 |
| Seattle | 24 |
| Tacoma | 43 |
| Preston | 6 |
| Fall City | 10 |
| Snoqualmie Falls | 14 |
| North Bend | 18 |
| Summit Snoqualmie Pass | 42 |
| Lake Sammamish | 3½ |
| Beaver Lake | 5 |
| Black Diamond | 16 |
| Hobart | 10 |
| Cle Elum | 75 |
| Wenatchee | 150 |
| Ellensburg | 106 |
| Yakima | 160 |
| Kent | 19 |
| Auburn | 25 |
| Lake McDonald | 6 |
| Pine Lake | 5 |
| Kerriston | 18 |
| Kirkland | 17 |
| Redmond | 12 |

Patronize the Advertisers Who Made This Folder Possible

Headquarters for
**MEATS, FISH and POULTRY**
Highest Market Price Paid for Live Stock
We Aim to Please You. If We Do, Tell Your Friends, If Not—
**Tell J. W. FINNEY**

"The Place to Meet Your Friends"
**LEW'S PLACE**
Soft Drinks, Confections, Ice Cream and Sandwiches
L. C. Lundberg. Prop.

**PRESTON-ISSAQUAH-SEATTLE AUTO STAGE**
Daily Schedule:
Daily except Saturday and Sunday—
Leave—
Preston ............. 8.15 am  2.00 pm
High Point ........ 8.25 am  2.10 pm
Issaquah .......... 8.30 am  2.15 pm
Coalfield .......... 8.45 am  2.30 pm
Renton ............. 9.00 am  2.45 pm
Leave—
Seattle ............. 10.00 am  5.00 pm
Renton ............. 10.40 am  5.40 pm
Coalfield .......... 10.55 am  5.55 pm
Issaquah .......... 11.10 am  6.10 pm
High Point ........ 11.15 am  6.15 pm
Saturday Only—
Leave—
Preston ... 8.15 am  2.00 pm  6.00 pm
High Point 8.25 am  2.10 pm  6.10 pm
Issaquah ..8.30 am  2.15 pm  6.15 pm
Coalfield ..8.45 am  2.30 pm  6.30 pm

"Outfitters For The Whole Family"
**LEONARD MILES**
General Merchandise    Fresh & Smoked Meats
Issaquah, Wash.

PROPERTY OF ISSAQUAH HISTORICAL SOCIETY

Sells Real Estate and Writes Fire Insurance
Issaquah, :: Washington

Renton ........9.00 am  2.45 pm  6.45 pm
Saturday Only—
Leave—
Seattle ....10.00 am  3.30 pm  7.45 pm
Renton ....10.40 am  4.10 pm  8.25 pm
Coalfield ..10.55 am  4.25 pm  8.40 pm
Issaquah ..11.10 am  4.40 pm  8.55 pm
High Point 11.15 am  4.45 pm  9.00 pm
Sunday Only—
Leave—
Preston ... 8.15 am  2.00 pm  8.00 pm
High Point  8.25 am  2.10 pm  8.10 pm
Issaquah .. 8.30 am  2.15 pm  8.15 pm
Coalfield .. 8.45 am  2.30 pm  8.30 pm
Renton .... 9.00 am  2.45 pm  8.45 pm
Leave—
Seattle ....10.00 am  6.00 pm  11.00 pm
Renton ....10.40 am  6.40 pm  11.40 pm
Coalfield ..10.55 am  6.55 pm  11.55 pm
Issaquah ..11.10 am  7.10 pm  12.10 am
High Point 11.15 am  7.15 pm  12.15 am

Pierce Arrow For Hire—Phone 332

**HEPLER MOTOR CO.**
*Ford*
PRODUCTS
Issaquah, Washington
8920.201

The Bank of Personal Service
**ISSAQUAH STATE BANK**
A. J. Peters, Cashier
Resources Over $400,000.00

**POCKET DIRECTORY**
and
**BOOSTER GUIDE**
—of—
**ISSAQUAH**
—
Souvenir of 1925 Rodeo
—
Compliments of Business Men

**A. L. WOLD COMPANY**
Building Material, Hardware, Paint, Glass, Wallpaper, Hay, Grain, Flour, Feed
Issaquah, Washington

▲ Labeled as a "Pocket Directory and Booster Guide of Issaquah," this handy souvenir brochure contains a wealth of information documenting a slice of life in 1920s Issaquah. Issaquah rodeos served as promotional events for local businesses and were held twice a year, on the Fourth of July and on Labor Day.  Issaquah Historical Society.

◄ Kaiser Paving Company employees are shown hard at work paving King County's Auburn-Enumclaw Road, ca. 1918. King County Archives.

Drivers proudly pose beside their Kirkland Transfer Company trucks in 1915. Kirkland Heritage Society. ►

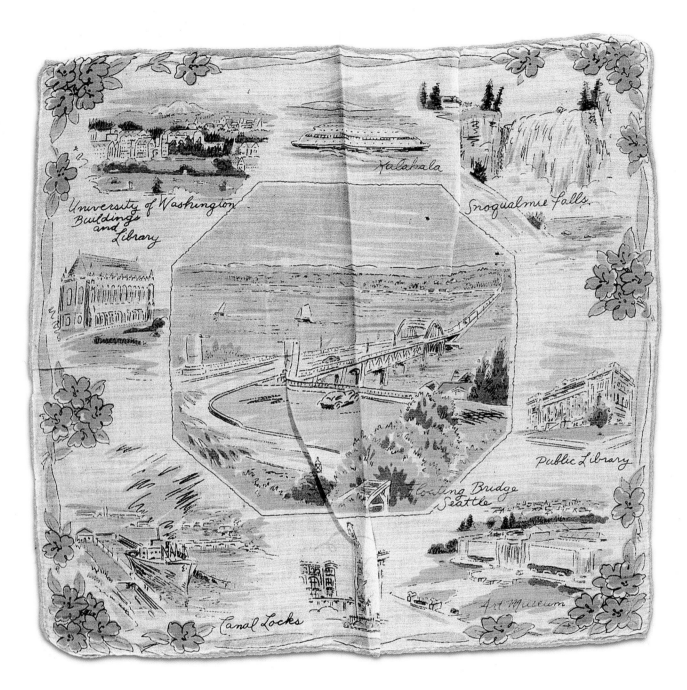

▲ A ca. 1950 souvenir handkerchief depicting greater Seattle landmarks gives the Lacey V. Murrow floating bridge center stage, and includes other transportation attractions such as the Hiram M. Chittenden Locks and the *Kalakala*. Eastside Heritage Center.

# By Air

Kenmore Air was constructed on land created by the 1916 lowering of Lake Washington due to the opening of the Hiram M. Chittenden Locks and the Ship Canal. Shown here in 1946 shortly after its founding, the company was the brainchild of Bob Munro, Reg Collins, and Jack Mines, three high school friends who reunited after World War II. What started as a one-airplane operation at the north end of Lake Washington has grown into the largest seaplane airline in the world. Kenmore Heritage Society. ▼

◄ Kenmore Air founder Bob Munro was the Northwest authority on floatplanes for more than half a century. He pioneered floatplane flights with the Aeronca Model K, Seabees and de Havilland Beavers and Otters. Photo courtesy Kenmore Air.

Located on the downtown Seattle waterfront, the Skinner & Eddy shipyard was merged with an adjacent yard formerly owned by Todd Shipyards in May 1918, the year of this photo. The Skinner & Eddy shipyard operated in Seattle during WWI, building cargo ships initially for export and then for the U.S. Shipping Board. Seattle's General Strike began with shipyard workers at Skinner & Eddy, which employed a majority of the nearly 30,000 shipyard workers in Seattle. More than 60,000 workers joined the General Strike, which ran from February 6 to February 11, 1919. Puget Sound Maritime Historical Society. ▼

# chapter six

# Making Community

*by Jim Compton*

Washington was different from the start, its politics eccentric and undisciplined, and its communities diverse and unpredictable. King County has often symbolized the state's rambunctious civic life.

One distinguished historian (Dorothy Johansen of Reed College) called Washington the home of "circus politics." The nation viewed the state, with some reason, as a hotbed of radical and utopian politics. Roosevelt's Postmaster General, James J. Farley once made a toast to "…the forty-seven states and the soviet of Washington."

If Oregon attracted staid farmers and urban burghers, Washington drew Wobblies and radical idealists. The Everett and Centralia Massacres and the Seattle General strike illustrate the often-dangerous political atmosphere. But Washington was also a leader in women's suffrage, industrial compensation, and direct legislation. John Dos Passos' book *Nineteen Nineteen* was modeled on the radical movements of the early 20th century around Puget Sound.

The state attracted an extraordinary number of utopian colonies, based on a communitarian ideal of pure democracy. Some who held property together were communistic; others who allowed personal property and individual profit would be called socialist today. The well-known Home Colony on south Puget Sound near Olympia had a reputation, probably justified, for nude bathing and free love. The famous anarchist Emma Goldman lectured

In 1877, the Sisters of Providence came to ▶ Seattle to operate the King County Poor Farm on the Duwamish River. Months later, in May of 1878, the sisters established the first Providence Hospital in a remodeled house on Fifth Avenue between Madison and Spring Streets. A second, larger hospital at the same site was built in several phases, beginning in 1882. Shown here in 1900 with streetcar tracks in the foreground, the hospital remained there until 1911, when it moved to 17th and Jefferson. In July of 1907 the Providence Hospital School of Nursing opened, with four lay students enrolled. The first class was graduated in 1910. Sisters of Providence Archives.

▲ George Bothell, for whom the town of Bothell is named, was a distinguished figure in his beaver top hat. The hat was part of his wardrobe during his term in the legislature in Olympia when Washington Territory became a state in 1889. Bothell Historical Museum Society.

▲ Small towns needed a general store and a local post office to survive. The ca. 1890 Montgomery Ward wheelbarrow was ordered from the catalog in the 1890s and used by Dick Tinnell to haul mail and produce through the town of Des Moines, providing necessary services to the community. Des Moines Historical Society.

at Home in 1898 on "the woman problem," although she later dismissed the colony as a place where people were "more interested in chickens and vegetables than propaganda."

In the thirties, the state elected a popular band leader, Vic Meyers, as Lieutenant Governor. Meyers' campaign slogan when he ran for mayor of Seattle was "A hostess in every streetcar."

The state's frisky pioneer spirit set the tone for the century that followed in King County. Organized labor held unusual sway, and Democratic Party politicians usually flourished in Western Washington's urban areas. Since the mid 1980s, King County has voted increasingly Democratic. Western King County, which includes Seattle, is a bastion of Democratic solidarity. Barack Obama whipped John McCain by 40% – the largest presidential margin in county history. It was King County that provided Democrat Maria Cantwell her slim majority over Senator Slade Gorton, and gave Christine Gregoire the votes for her razor-slim win over Republican Dino Rossi. In 2005 state government allowed the county to rename itself "Martin Luther King County."

It is not accidental that the 1990s saw a movement in rural East King County to secede. The campaign to create "Cedar County" was an angry reaction to the extension of land-use regulations to rural agricultural areas. The secession movement was revived in 2005 as "Cascade County." The drive to opt out of King County was both a manifestation of the contentious political atmosphere around progressive land-use policies, and a symptom of how rural areas view the democratic citadel of Seattle.

King County (and its immediate northern neighbor Everett) can claim to have produced two of the most effective politicians in recent American history, Warren Magnuson and Henry Jackson. Magnuson was a giant in liberal social legislation,

▲ From 1904 to 1934, the University of Washington held an annual Campus Day on which students and faculty worked together at a variety of tasks to improve the campus, and campus life. Two photos illustrate the type of activities accomplished on a typical Campus Day. With Denny Hall as a background, a group of volunteers on the first Campus Day in 1904 appear to be clearing a trench or drainage ditch across University of Washington property. University of Washington Libraries.

◄ The program advertises a fundraising event on May 17, 1909 at the Dreamland Pavilion to support Norway Day and Sangerfest Day at the Alaska-Yukon-Pacific Exposition, which was about to open on June 1. Many local organizations, such as the Norwegian Singing Societies of Greater Seattle, participated in the AYPE, and special "days" were assigned throughout the exposition to showcase various aspects of the Pacific Northwest. Dreamland Pavilion, located at Seventh and Union Streets in Seattle, was often the venue for fundraisers, competitions and dances. Nordic Heritage Museum.

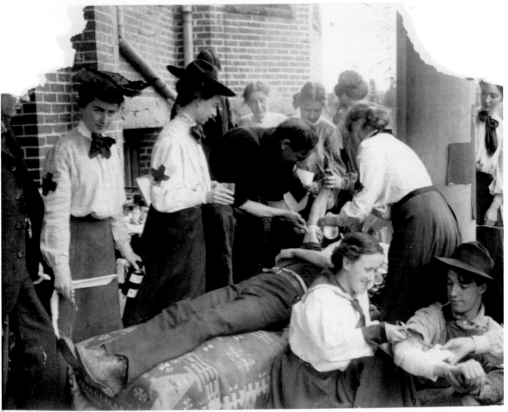

◄ Campus Day in 1905 included a disaster preparedness exercise, with students playing the parts of both victims and nurses. University of Washington Libraries.

and brought billions of federal dollars home to the state. Jackson was a domestic liberal, but a ferocious foreign policy hawk and critic of the Soviet Union. He made two runs for president, and was widely considered a favorite in 1976, when tactical errors lost him the nomination to Jimmy Carter.

Our community life has been loud and boisterous from the start. If the past is key to the present, we can find the roots of King County's (and Seattle's) penchant for argument and seemingly endless political process in Washington's wild early political history. We are comfortable with – and entertained by – political theater in our civic life.

---

*Jim Compton is an Oregon native and Reed College graduate. He was the Cairo and London correspondent for NBC News, and he hosted the Compton Report on Seattle's KING-TV for ten years. Later, Compton served on the Seattle City Council. Now he is writing a book on Oregon's Modoc Indian War.*

Maintaining communications between neighbors in rural communities became easier as telephone lines became available in the early 1900s. A single operator could connect dozens of calls a day from a manual switchboard such as this. Des Moines Historical Society. ▼

◄ The Pacific Northwest became well-known for its fruit orchards early in its territorial history, and the 1909 Alaska-Yukon-Pacific Exposition showcased Washington's excellent produce and community harvests. An expression of the community effort that went into the harvest is the cider-pressing parties that happened wherever apple trees grew. This early 20th century wooden cider press from Maple Valley was used in local orchards to create the juice base for cider and vinegar. Maple Valley Historical Society.

The first Swedish Hospital, shown here around 1915, was founded in 1910 by Dr. Nils Johanson, a surgeon and Swedish immigrant. It began as a small nonprofit hospital in a renovated apartment building, with just 24 beds to serve the surrounding communities. Nordic Heritage Museum. ►

◄ Labor union "Labor Day" ribbons were worn proudly in 1912 by unionized Black Diamond area miners. Black Diamond Historical Society.

A wheelchair from the early days of Swedish Hospital gives silent testimony to the hospital's long history of service. Nordic Heritage Museum. ►

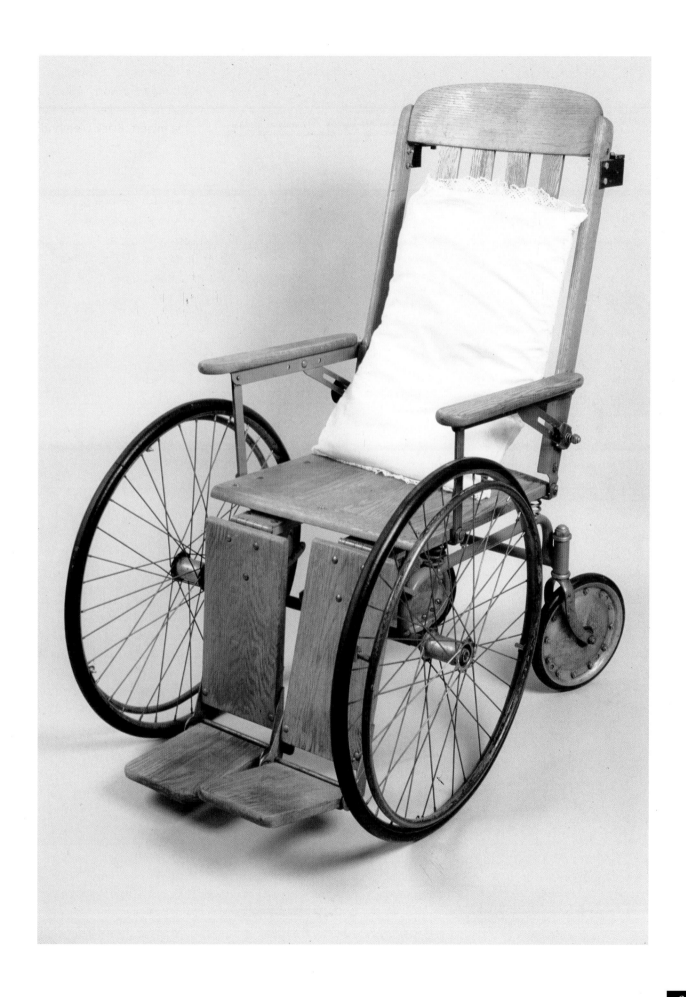

▲ The Draper Children's Home in Des Moines took in orphans and taught them music and work skills. Here, the Home's Orchestra poses in 1915 for a photo. Des Moines Historical Society.

In 1889, two months before Washington Territories achieved statehood, the Washington State Grange was established to assist the state's farmers in cooperative buying and selling, in political action, and in the creation of strong communities. The 1920 Washington State Grange handbook contains the articles of incorporation and bylaws of the Grange Wholesale Warehouse Company. Enumclaw Plateau Historical Society. ▶

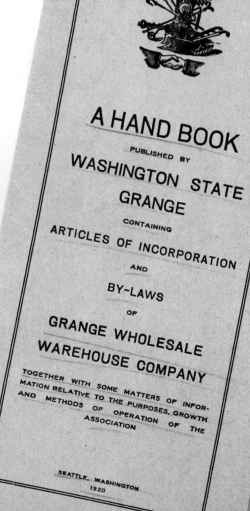

A HAND BOOK
PUBLISHED BY
WASHINGTON STATE GRANGE
CONTAINING
ARTICLES OF INCORPORATION
AND
BY-LAWS
OF
GRANGE WHOLESALE WAREHOUSE COMPANY
TOGETHER WITH SOME MATTERS OF INFORMATION RELATIVE TO THE PURPOSES, GROWTH AND METHODS OF OPERATION OF THE ASSOCIATION

SEATTLE, WASHINGTON
1920

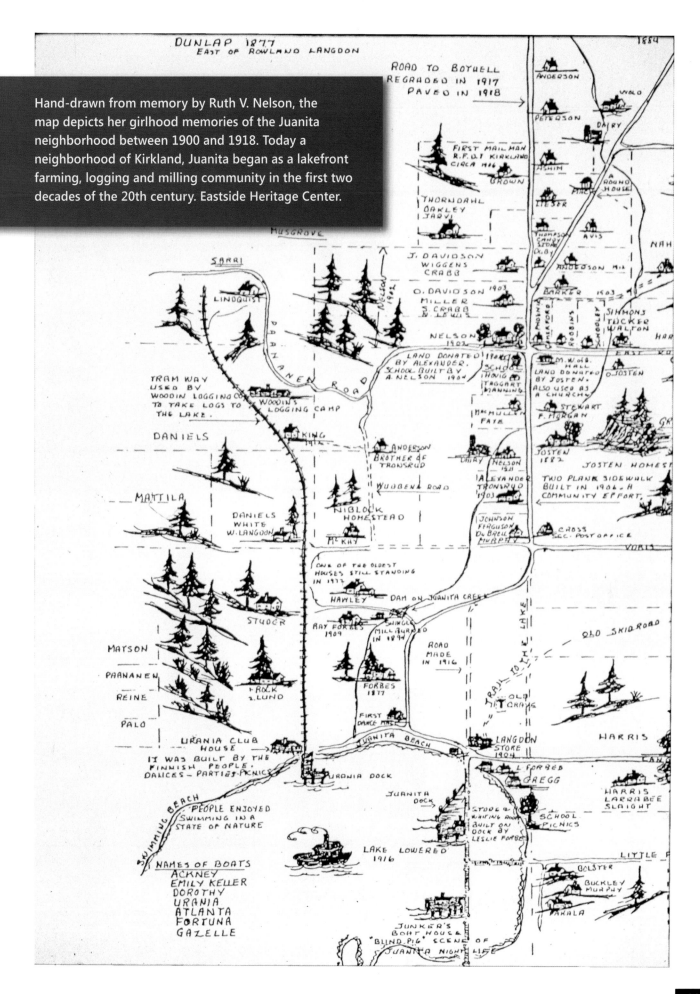

Hand-drawn from memory by Ruth V. Nelson, the map depicts her girlhood memories of the Juanita neighborhood between 1900 and 1918. Today a neighborhood of Kirkland, Juanita began as a lakefront farming, logging and milling community in the first two decades of the 20th century. Eastside Heritage Center.

▲ Taken on the steps of the Seattle Welsh Presbyterian Church, the Welsh Ladies Aid is pictured in 1920. Puget Sound Welsh Organization.

▲ Mrs. Flora Hartwell started the lunch program at Broadview School. She prepared food at home and brought it to the school in a 1921 "Lizzie" Ford Touring Car with the help of her five-year-old son, George. The 1926 photo captures her carrying out her appointed task. Broadview Historical Society.

In 1950, three men in Maple Valley signed a $1000 note to purchase the 1926 Howard Cooper fire engine, the first fire engine in the Valley. The first day on the job, the engine and crew responded to two calls: at the Finnish bathhouse in Hobart and to a house fire. After the Maple Valley Volunteer Fire Department became King County Fire Dist. #43, the Howard Cooper was sold in 1955. Eventually it was abandoned and most of its brass was stolen. In 1969, it was purchased back by the volunteer firefighters who spent 6000 hours to restore it. Maple Valley Historical Society.

◄

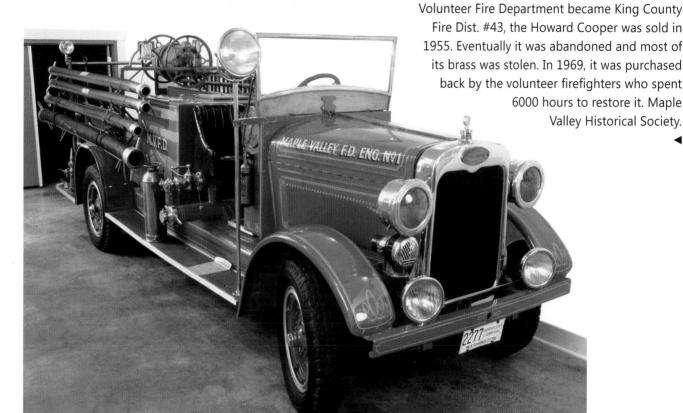

◄ Photographed soon after opening, the Burien Co-operative Store was started in 1921, selling necessities at reasonable prices. Highline Historical Society.

The constant conflict between the law and lawbreakers is depicted ca. 1920 as police break up gambling machines in Seattle. As the city grew, so did its challenge to keep the community safe and law-abiding. Museum of History & Industry. ▶

Seattle, Washington
1978 - 1979

Queen Anne Garden Club

◀ The Queen Anne Garden Club was founded in 1939 as part of a movement to beautify the Queen Anne neighborhood. The Queen Anne neighborhood is centered on Queen Anne Hill, which is 463 feet in height and two miles north of downtown Seattle. The yearbook shown was hand-created by the garden club for the 1978-79 year. Queen Anne Historical Society.

◄ This rare copy of *Black Square and Compass: 200 Years of Prince Hall Freemasonry* by Joseph A. Wilkes, Jr., 1975, documents the Prince Hall Masons, first organized in 1775 among free blacks in Boston, Massachusetts. The Seattle branch of the Prince Hall Masons met in the lodge at 23rd Avenue and Madison Street. Black Heritage Society of Washington State.

▲ This campaign sign for Wing Luke, Seattle City Council, was printed for the 1961 election. Wing Luke was the first Asian American to be elected to public office in the Pacific Northwest. He was elected to the Seattle City Council in 1962 and served until his death in 1965. Wing Luke Asian Museum.

▲ Properly known as the Gardner Shackle, but popularly known as the "Oregon Boot," the restraint was patented in 1866 by Oregon State Penitentiary Warden J.C. Gardner. These heavily weighted shackles were manufactured at the penitentiary by prisoners and used to prevent prisoners from escape. The model in this picture is from about 1930. Seattle Metropolitan Police Museum.

# chapter seven

# Education

*by Patricia Filer*

The unmistakable smell of mothballs permeated the air as the dry cleaner's plastic sheet slipped over the hook of the old wooden hanger. By today's standards, the dark blue letterman's sweater looked impossibly small to belong to a high school athlete. On the right pocket was a simple block letter adorned with a small embroidered football. The octogenarian caressed the faded yellow W gently before raising his moist blue eyes to his friends at the museum get-together.

Then, smiling proudly, he announced in a quiet and tremulous voice, "West Seattle Indians, Class of '42." Creased faces smiled back and after a respectful and thoughtful silence, excited voices began to recall personal experiences of other glorious pigskin seasons, escalating in volume and excitement. Then, one by one, others carefully unwrapped precious mementos that they had brought to the school-artifact gathering…medals, trophies, gym uniforms, fragile and yellowing report cards, programs from plays or musical events, photographs, and yearbooks.

For several hours, unique and irreplaceable memories from days long-past circulated freely and were carefully documented by museum staff. Unguarded and spontaneous recollections from community elders unlocked honest and unique views into that community's past. Education is the key to a deeply rooted and commonly shared experience. Yet for some, the exercise of reliving school days can be bittersweet.

This area's early pioneer families each included school–aged children. The Alki Landing party had 12 children – all under the age of eight; the Duwamish Valley party had two. Along their

One of the last reunions of the Territorial University of Washington's first graduating class featured several notable people from the early days of Seattle. Those pictured in this 1892 photo are: Edward S. Buckling, Sarah L. Denny, Edgar Bryan, Alice Mercer, Susanna Mercer, Martha Craw and Margaret Denny. Daughters of the Pioneers of Washington State. ▼

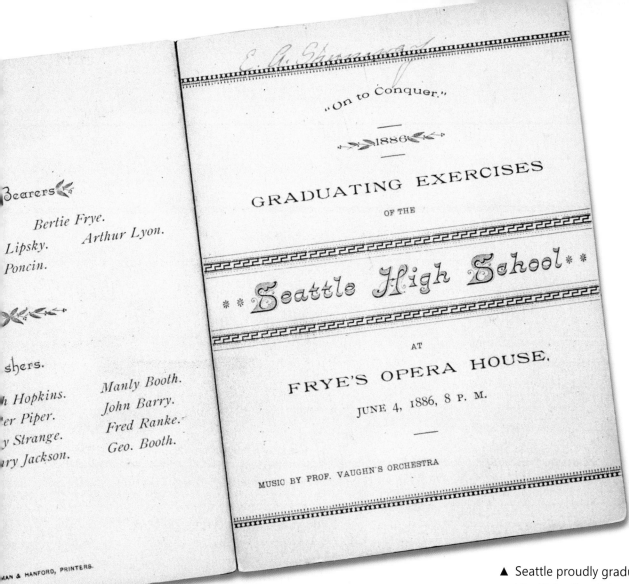

E. A. Shumway

"On to Conquer."

1886

GRADUATING EXERCISES

OF THE

**Seattle High School**

AT

FRYE'S OPERA HOUSE,

JUNE 4, 1886, 8 P. M.

MUSIC BY PROF. VAUGHN'S ORCHESTRA

Bearers

Bertie Frye.

Lipsky.        Arthur Lyon.

Poncin.

shers.

Hopkins.        Manly Booth.
er Piper.        John Barry.
y Strange.        Fred Ranke.
ary Jackson.        Geo. Booth.

MAN & HANFORD, PRINTERS.

▲ Seattle proudly graduated its first public high school class in 1886, documented in the commencement program from Seattle High School. Emma Shumway, whose signature appears on the program, taught at the school. She came to Seattle in 1884 with ten years of teaching experience and taught at Seattle High School until 1903. Seattle Public Schools Archive.

◄ Built in 1885, Bothell's first school was a one-room affair that housed grades one through eight. Initially located on Main Street, the building was converted into a residence in 1890 and relocated to the park at Bothell Landing, as shown here, in 1989. Bothell Historical Museum Society.

arduous trips to the Pacific Northwest, most of these youngsters received their education from peers or parents whenever there was a spare moment. Precious family Bibles were used as readers when primers and other school materials were discarded to reduce weight on covered wagons. Everyday tasks such as determining how much to feed the animals, how many teaspoons of sugar could be spared for a recipe – or more importantly – how much farther is it until we get to Oregon? – became practical math lessons. Letters were traced in the dust along the trail.

One of the first matters of business for the founding families after they had constructed their homesteads was to establish schools for the children and to find suitable teachers. Young John Wesley Maple was installed as the first teacher in the Duwamish Valley even though he had only had four years of school himself. Even though school terms were only in session for three months in spring and three months in the fall, Maple was quoted as saying it was the hardest job he had ever undertaken.

In 1864, Seattle resident Asa Mercer recruited a group of 11 young women from the East Coast to serve as teachers for the young settlement. They were known as "the Mercer Girls," and it was widely speculated that they were really encouraged to come to Washington Territory in order to alleviate the shortage of women in the Puget Sound area. Historical documents, photographs, and family histories have preserved this chapter of the county's early education history.

For thousands of years, the children of local Native American tribes that inhabited this area learned life's lessons by means of long-standing oral traditions which were passed down from generation to generation. As the First People were forced from their lands, many Indian children of this region were forced to attend mission schools in an attempt to erase their culture. In recent years, oral histories have been conducted with Native American elders to collect and safeguard those

▲ The 1910 photo of the Horace Mann Grammar School baseball team is taken from the 1916-1921 five-year report of Seattle Public Schools Board of Directors. In addition to the regular gymnasium, provision was made for athletics for both girls and boys throughout the school districts in King County, as exemplified in the 1911 girls basketball team from Rainier Valley High School. Seattle Public Schools Archive, and Rainier Valley Historical Society.

Redmond High School football team, ca. 1915.
Lake Washington School District. ▼

◄ The two-story Maple
Valley School building, with
daylight basement, was
built in 1920 and was in use
as a school for 50 years.
Designated an Historical
Landmark, it currently
houses the Maple Valley
Historical Museum.  Maple
Valley Historical Society.

unique customs and distinctive Coast Salish languages that had not been lost or forgotten.

Japanese American teachers and students were forced to leave behind homes and classmates when they were sent to internment camps following the attack on Pearl Harbor. Heartbreaking photos, handwritten memoirs, and first-hand recollections have been preserved as compelling reminders of this painful chapter in the history of King County education.

As Seattle continued to grow, there was increased discrimination in housing, which resulted in schools becoming increasingly segregated. Most students of color lived and attended school in the Central District – an inner city area just south of downtown. As a general rule, predominantly non-white schools got fewer resources from the district than those with a predominantly white population. It was not until 1947 that the Seattle Public Schools hired its first black teachers and not until 1968 that the district began to promote integration by converting Garfield High School into the city's first "magnet school." From 1978 to 1997, the Seattle School District implemented a mandatory busing plan in an attempt to achieve racial balance in local middle schools. While local municipal and school archives contain the public records and administrative documents which illustrate this period in our education history, much is learned from the recorded first-hand recollections of students.

In a little over 150 years, King County's population has grown from those few hardy pioneer families to more than two million people – over 20 percent of them school-aged. Approximately a quarter of the students enrolled in King County schools represent diverse ethnic groups, and providing a first-class education for each child has remained a priority. Protecting and preserving the history of this educational evolution has become an important mission of local historical societies and museums and they have become safety deposit boxes for school artifacts and memories. The provenance of these treasures reveals important

Camp Fire Girls taught respect for, and broad imitation ▶ of, Native American culture. The young woman dressed in pseudo-Indian garb would likely have researched and sewn her own ceremonial clothing, ca. 1920. Camp Fire was not all about ceremony, however, and taught groups of girls useful things outside of the traditional classroom, such as leadership skills and giving back to the community. Camp Fire Museum. ▲

insights into other ethnic and cultural events taking place both in King County and in the rest of the world.

*Patricia Filer has served as the Education Director for HistoryLink.org for the past five years. She has written award-winning curricula and maintains and coordinates all of HistoryLink's education projects including grant managing, educational outreach, and all content found in the Education Resource. Pat served as 4Culture Heritage Education and Special Projects Program Manager from 2007-2009. She was the Director of West Seattle's Log House Museum from 1997-2004. Pat is an active member of Association of King County Historical Organizations (AKCHO), Southwest Seattle Historical Society, Friends of Georgetown History, and Washington Museum Association (WMA).*

While urban Asian neighborhoods have had some success at maintaining cultural continuity, families scattered in rural communities or in neighborhoods not predominantly Asian have maintained language and culture through classes for their children. This reader was used for learning the Chinese language at the Chong Wa Chinese school for children of immigrants. Wing Luke Asian Museum. ▶

A combined class of first- and second-graders at St. Catherine School in 1943 is watched over by Sister Miriam Kathleen. The younger students are practicing their penmanship while the second graders are reading. The Sisters of Providence opened St. Catherine in 1941 and withdrew from teaching there in 1975. Sisters of Providence Archive. ▼

中華民國教育部審定
美洲華僑小學教科書
# 國語
高級第一冊

正中書局印行

小高／3

# chapter eight

# Worship

*by Olaf Kvamme*

The Duwamish tribe of Native Americans, which inhabited the land now called King County, were not worshippers of any supreme being nor were they seemingly interested in creation or cosmology. They honored the land, and believed in the immortality of certain animals. They also believed the well-being of an individual depended on the intercession of a guardian spirit.

Protestant and Catholic churches as well as synagogues sprang up around the county. Seattle's first church was built in 1855. The Little White Church was where the Methodist Episcopalians worshiped.  Ten years later, Episcopalians began worshiping at Trinity Church. The first Catholic church in Seattle was Our Lady of Good Help, founded in 1869 and guided by Fr. Francis Xavier Prefontaine.

As Scandinavians began to make their homes here, they founded Protestant churches, nostalgically naming some after the homes they'd left behind, and they continued to worship in their native language.

Early in the 20th century Jewish residents established synagogues for both Ashkenazic and Sephardic congregations, which now number over 21. As new immigrants arrived in King County, in many instances they worshipped in vacated churches and synagogues.

The word worship has various definitions among the bodies which have come to be known as members of the faith community.

## Christian

The Christian Endeavor Convention poster, printed by General Litho and Printing Company, Seattle, promoted the 23rd annual international convention held in Seattle in 1907. The unknown artist created a romanticized portrait of Seattle, Elliott Bay and Mt. Rainier as seen from a fictional promontory occupied by a pseudo-Native American man dressed in a baptismal robe. A rendering of the famous Tlingit totem pole stolen from Fort Tongass, Alaska, and erected in Pioneer Square in 1899 stands behind the man as he gazes meaningfully into the distance. Washington State Historical Society. ▼

## Jewish

◄ The Tallit, or Prayer Shawl, is a four-cornered fringed religious garment donned by Jewish men during the morning prayers in the synagogue. Washington State Jewish Historical Society.

Worn in Seattle in the early 20th century, the Tallit was kept in its own carrier, the Tallit Bag. Washington State Jewish Historical Society. ▼

Social services have become one of the ways of worship in these communities, and nowhere is it evidenced more than by the Salvation Army, an evangelical part of the universal Christian Church.

Attention to health and education has been a focus of the Catholic Church with the establishment of Cabrini and Providence Hospitals in Seattle and Seattle University. Catholic Community Services provides many essential services to the community and its adoption program has been placing children for adoption since 1937.

The Jewish faith community has offered social services to its members since its first formation. The American Moslem Foundation has been formed as a charitable non-profit organization with participation open to all Muslims from various denominations. The Foundation's Covington-based House of Mercy projects include a cemetery which accommodates the needs for the availability of Islamic ritual funeral services and cemeteries and is also is involved in the development of education facilities.

Homes for the elderly such as Horizon House, Parkshore and Hearthstone are sponsored by the United Church of Christ, Presbyterian and Lutheran communities. Other examples of basic service include showers and other physical comforts made available at the Compass Mission in the Pioneer Square area of Seattle, and laundry facilities at the Immanuel Lutheran Church in Seattle.

Worship institutions have also been active promoters of civil rights. During the 1960s and 1970s, the Reverend Samuel B. McKinney of the Mount Zion Baptist Church and the Reverend John H. Adams of the First African Methodist Episcopal Church occupied particularly prominent leadership roles.

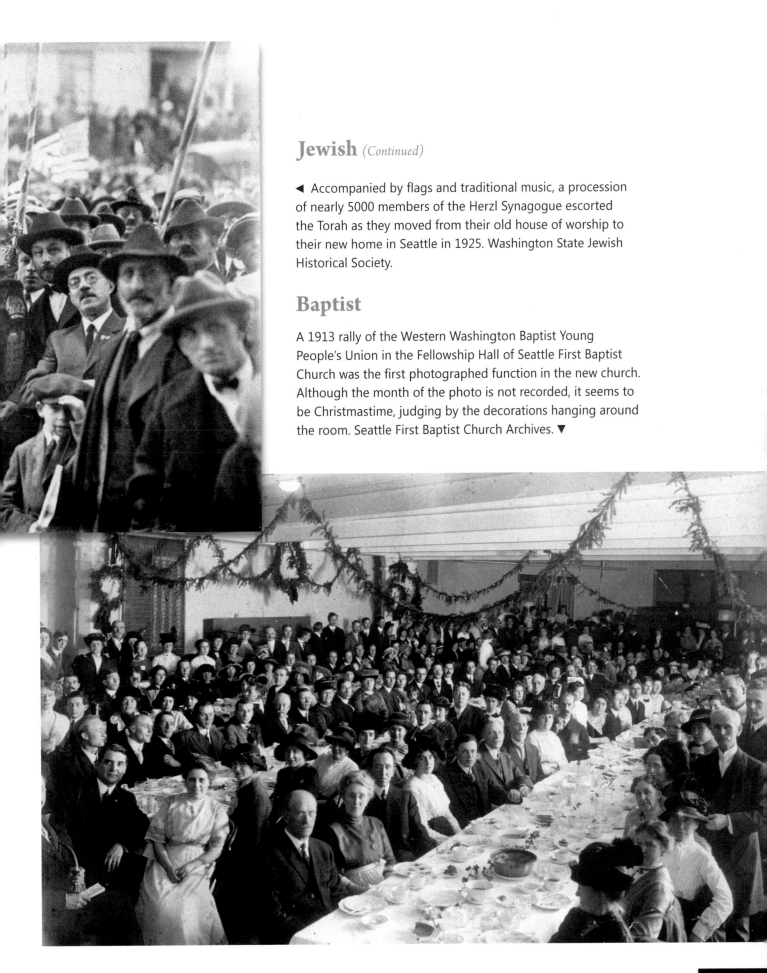

## Jewish *(Continued)*

◀ Accompanied by flags and traditional music, a procession of nearly 5000 members of the Herzl Synagogue escorted the Torah as they moved from their old house of worship to their new home in Seattle in 1925. Washington State Jewish Historical Society.

## Baptist

A 1913 rally of the Western Washington Baptist Young People's Union in the Fellowship Hall of Seattle First Baptist Church was the first photographed function in the new church. Although the month of the photo is not recorded, it seems to be Christmastime, judging by the decorations hanging around the room. Seattle First Baptist Church Archives. ▼

In recent years new social needs have caught the attention of faith communities. Environmental concerns are supported by Earth Ministries Greening Congregations. Homeless people find refuge in tent cities throughout the county on church property and some church kitchens are devoted to preparing meals for the poor. Trinity Parish in Seattle has been a leader in the Neighbors in Need program, which provides food in bulk for families.

These examples of social service-related contributions made by worship sources provide an overview of the extensive role that they play beyond their primary role of worship. Most of the worship institutions will indicate that their social service is part of worship.

Photographs, papers and other ephemera which document the way of worship can be found in the museums and historical societies of King County.

*Olaf Kvamme was a Seattle School Administrator, President of the Nordic Heritage Museum Board and Chair of the Bergen Sister City Committee. As a member of the Territory of Washington Sesquicentennial Commission he researched the churches in the state that worshipped in Scandinavian language prior to statehood and this resulted in an exhibit and establishment of an impressive archive at the Nordic Heritage Museum.*

◀ On February 26, 1920, photographer Asahel Curtis captured for posterity Elder W.D. Carter and other elders of the Mount Zion Baptist Church, one of Seattle's oldest Black churches. The location is likely the church on 11th and Union, built in 1907. The occasion for the photo is unknown, but it may be significant that less than two months later, in April of 1920, the church broke ground at 19th and Madison for a new brick building. Washington State Historical Society.

The program dated December 23, 1917 features an image of Seattle First Baptist Church at the corner of Harvard and Seneca. Seattle First Baptist Church Archives. ▶

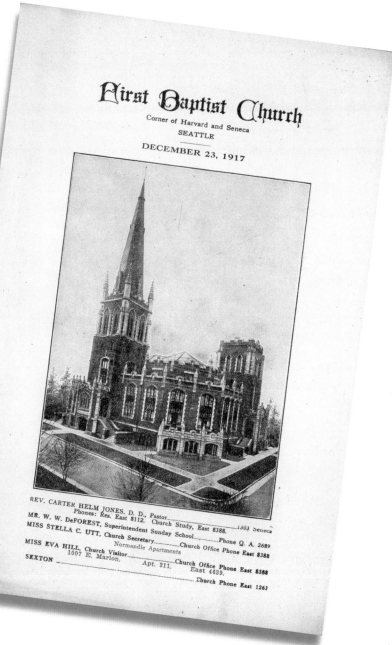

First Baptist Church
Corner of Harvard and Seneca
SEATTLE

DECEMBER 23, 1917

REV. CARTER HELM JONES, D. D., Pastor_____1303 Seneca
Phones: Res. East 8112. Church Study, East 8388.
MR. W. W. DeFOREST, Superintendent Sunday School.
MISS STELLA C. UTT, Church Secretary_____Phone Q. A. 2689
Normandie Apartments_____Church Office Phone East 8388
MISS EVA HILL, Church Visitor.
1007 E. Marion.       Apt. 311.____Church Office Phone East 8388
SEXTON _____East 4639.
_____Church Phone East 1263

◄ A twelve-page booklet with cover photo by Asahel Curtis features Seattle First Baptist Church Education Hall in 1930. The building was constructed in 1906 as Minor Hospital, at 1420 Spring Street, commemorating early Seattle mayor, T.T. Minor, who died in 1889. Minor Hospital was a state-of-the-art 45-bed private hospital with a maternity ward. The First Baptist Church bought the property in 1930, renaming the building Education Hall. Seattle First Baptist Church Archives.

*Kennydale Baptist Church after printing*

Photographed by a local studio on July 21, 1940, the First Baptist Church in Kennydale shows off a fresh coat of paint. The church served as a community center and a place of worship for Black families in the Renton area, where African-American miners had been recruited to work the coal mines of southeast King County. Black Heritage Society of Washington State.

An unknown photographer in 1970 captured a moment of dance during the Bon Odori Festival in Seattle. The Obon is a traditional Japanese festival that marks respect for ancestors. While many immigrants from Japan adopted religions not native to Japan, they also retained long-held traditions, some of which are related to Buddhist practices. Wing Luke Asian Museum. ▶

## Buddhist

This is one of the last photos to be taken of the original Seattle Buddhist Temple at 1020 Main Street in 1939, before it was condemned and torn down that year to make way for the Yesler Terrace housing project. Seattle Buddhist Temple.

## Catholic

◄ The decorative element from the chasuble of Mary is known as a "Marian detail." Archives of the Archdiocese of Seattle.

The black and silver chasuble (or vestment) and matching stole were worn by Catholic priests during Mass celebrations at the St. Thomas seminary, located on Lake Washington in the city of Kenmore. Originally called St. Edward Seminary in 1931 when it opened, it became St. Thomas Seminary in 1958, and closed in 1977. Archives of the Archdiocese of Seattle. ►

Virtually unchanged for over 100 years, the habit was worn by members of the Sisters of Providence religious community from 1844 until 1966, when a modified habit was adopted. The habit included a silver pectoral cross and a set of Our Lady of Seven Dolors, or Sorrows – beads suspended from the waist. A separate rosary contains seven decades, or bead sets, rather than the standard ten of most rosaries. Sisters of Providence Archives. ▶

## Presbyterian

The First Presbyterian Church of Brighton Beach, King County, Washington was formally organized on September 17, 1901. Services were held in a tent at first, seen in this photo of the tent's interior. The cornerstone was laid for a wood-frame church on July 4, 1902 at Rainier Avenue and Brighton, and the new building was dedicated November 15, 1903. Its name was changed to Brighton Presbyterian Church in 1988. Rainier Valley Historical Society. ▶

The new Seattle Welsh Presbyterian Church, its image recorded for posterity on a postcard, was built in 1907 at 10th Avenue E and E John Street after the congregation outgrew the original 1893 building on Olive Way. The photo inset is of J. Michael Hughes, who was pastor of the church from 1891-1894 and from 1905-1912. The activities of Seattle's Welsh residents were centered around their church, and many lived within a mile of its doorstep. The Presbytery called for the church's demolition in 1956, and with it went many of the records that documented its parishioners and the Welsh community's contributions to the area. Puget Sound Welsh Association. ▼

## Other

In this photo, ca. 1931, a humbly constructed church serves the spiritual needs of the residents of Hooverville, the shantytown that sprang up just south of downtown Seattle during the Great Depression. Washington State Historical Society.

# chapter nine

# Industry

*by Leonard Garfield*

In a nation whose traditions evoke an agrarian ideal and in a region whose natural bounty suggests an untamed wilderness, it is easy to forget that the first American settlers imagined King County as the setting for an industrial future.

"Come at once," 19-year-old David Denny implored his family as he stood on the desolate shores of Puget Sound in 1851, "there is room for 1,000." With those words, Denny articulated a shared vision that a metropolis would arise, King County would be a destination for rail lines crossing the continent, and the industrial revolution would reach and transform the frontier.

Denny didn't wait long. The transformation began nearly at once in the unlikely guise of Henry Yesler, an itinerant entrepreneur who in 1852 convinced the settlers to donate land so that he could build a steam-powered sawmill, harvest the timberlands that hemmed them in, and lay a skid road between.

That these youthful pioneers agreed to an old stranger's audacious proposal might have seemed risky. But it was a decision that set King County apart from its Puget Sound rivals and by March 1853, when Yesler's mill sawed its first plank, nearly everyone in town either worked for him or sold him timber, and ships loaded King County planks and pilings bound for San Francisco, the Philippines and beyond. The industrial frontier had arrived.

From that beginning, King County experienced an industrial trajectory nearly unparalleled in American history. The extraction of natural resources – timber, coal, even fish – soon led to industrial processing

▲ Built as a hobby farm by Frederick Spencer Stimson in 1910, the Hollywood Farm near Woodinville became a model of scientific dairy management. Stimson later diversified his model farm, raising poultry and pigs, and growing produce in industrial-sized greenhouses said to be the most modern west of the Mississippi. Woodinville Historical Society.

# Farming

The Dougherty farmhouse, outbuildings and barn are located at Cherry Valley Road in Duvall and are some of the oldest standing structures in the Snoqualmie River Valley. Built in 1888, the wood-frame house has been restored, complete with furnishings such as its wood cooking stove. The farmstead was designated an historic site in 1983. Duvall Historical Society. ▼

on a vast scale – milling, refining, butchering – and then to the manufacturing that placed the region in the front ranks of the American economy.

The transformation happened at blinding speed. By the turn of the century and in the decades after, King County mills led the nation in timber production. Coal from King County mines powered the American West. An industrial agricultural economy – large scale dairies, breweries, food processing plants – served a vast economic hinterland. Iron and steel mills grew to serve the mills and factories. And an infrastructure of rail, sail and labor connected a growing network of mill towns and industrial cities and ports.

It was not a straightforward path, of course. The industrial frontier was vulnerable to the booms and busts of economic cycles. Heavily dependent on extractive industries and distant capital, King County was hit hard by the economic dips of the 19th century, and mired in the depths of a national depression in the 1890s. As the century wound down, businesses closed, workers lost jobs, and plants were shuttered.

But as if Horatio Alger himself wrote the script, depression met fortune in 1897 with the news that gold from the Klondike had arrived in Seattle. The stories of gold shook King County to its core, but the real transformation happened in its industrial base. Entrepreneurs like Robert Moran and Joshua Green built fleets of ships to carry miners and supplies between King County and the goldfields. The ensuing wealth begat more industry. In 1904, Moran Brothers shipyard built the USS *Nebraska*, a mighty steel-hulled battleship that placed King County shipbuilding on equal footing with the great shipyards of the East Coast.

Within the decade, tens of thousands were employed in the region's shipyards, and hundreds of ships were built – a milestone that put Seattle into the league of great manufacturing cities. In the years that followed, clothing manufacture,

▲ The Golden Arrow Dairy, located at what is today 65th and Southcenter Boulevard in Tukwila, was one of dozens of small local dairies once scattered throughout King County in the early to mid-1900s. Tukwila Historical Society.

In 1937, George Thompsen turned a Depression-era hobby of growing blueberries into a business that was shipping 40 tons of berries annually by 1954. The 1945 blueberry syrup box from "Wild Cliffe Farm" represents one of the products from Thompsen's enterprise. Kenmore Heritage Society. ▶

After hops, dairy farming was the second major agricultural venture in Issaquah. Pressed or molded paper caps were used to seal glass milk bottles. Issaquah Historical Society. ▼

automobile production, railcar and truck factories all grew under the stimulus of plentiful labor, good transportation, and readily available materials – and the introduction of large-scale hydroelectricity.

If manufacturing added value to the basic processing, technology added value to manufacturing in the early 20th century. In the run-up to American involvement in World War I, William Boeing's young company employed local materials and maritime craftsmen but introduced new technology, building training planes for the Navy; after the war, pilot Eddie Hubbard convinced a skeptical Boeing that the future might well lay in a novel commercial application – carrying mail by air. It was the start of a manufacturing empire and provided a technological basis to the King County economy.

The shift from an unskilled to technological work force was neither easy nor smooth. The fundamental economic structure of King County remained unchanged through the early 20th century – a large working class (much of it unskilled), a significant transient population, and a vulnerability to national economic trends. The General Strike of 1919 and the catastrophic effects of the Great Depression were reminders that even as the region grew it was impacted by forces beyond its control.

But in the years of World War II and beyond, King County harnessed local industry to international circumstances. In the wake of Pearl Harbor, King County changed almost overnight from a community of reluctant isolationists into the classic home front city. Boeing jumpstarted to the front ranks of American industry; the region attracted workers from across the nation to work in King County defense industries; and the industrial workforce could claim with justice that it helped achieve victory.

Not only did Boeing, Paccar and the shipyards build the machines that would win the war, they transformed King County. Suddenly, thousands of unskilled workers were re-trained and better able to afford a middle-class lifestyle that prized education,

# Logging

The Snoqualmie Falls Lumber Company was at the forefront of technology when it began using an electric chainsaw in 1944. The chainsaw was powered by a generator mounted on caterpillar tractor treads. However, the downside was that fallers were often shocked by stray electrical currents during wet weather. The chain was oiled with recycled logging-truck engine oil. Snoqualmie Valley Historical Society. ▼

◀ Built in 1936 on 244th near the Redmond-Fall City Road, the Henry Isaacson Mill began as a private enterprise meant for family projects, but soon began to supply lumber to the community. Lumber from the mill was used in many of the resorts in the Pine Lake area of Sammamish in cabins, docks and diving boards. The mill is still owned and operated by Henry's son, Duane Isaacson. Sammamish Heritage Society.

▲ Owned by father and son A.P. Merideth and C.O. Merideth,
◀ The Merideth Lumber Company used both horses and a small railroad for their logging operation. Averaging 12,000 board-feet per day during their reign in the Kent area in the early 1900s, most of their lumber was shipped by rail to Seattle. Greater Kent Historical Society images.

recreation and the natural environment. In part, the transformation was possible because the work force was designing and building the most complex technological products of the age.

For the next five decades, King County's new technological workforce innovated its way to commercial success. When test pilot Tex Johnston flew the Dash 80, prototype of the Boeing 707, into a breathtaking barrel roll over Lake Washington in 1955, his spectacular display celebrated the engineering feats of the region and helped launched the jet age. In the decades that followed, the county's industrial base grew increasingly diverse and technologically sophisticated, leading by century's end to a new industrial order, dominated by Microsoft and other powerhouses of the digital age. But in some respects, that new economy was the culmination of changes unleashed when Yesler's mill first staked a claim on the industrial frontier.

---

*Leonard Garfield earned his M.A. in American Culture from the University of Michigan. He joined the Museum of History & Industry as Executive Director in 1999. Previously he served as manager of the King County Office of Cultural Resources from 1993 until 1999, where he oversaw the programs of the King County Arts Commission and King County Landmarks and Heritage Commission. From 1985 until 1993 Garfield was manager of Historic Preservation Programs for the State of Washington. He was Preservation Historian for the State Historical Society of Wisconsin from 1981 to 1985.*

Around 1900, an unknown photographer captured for posterity a pair of loggers, presumably "Bill and Jack," resting on a fallen tree with Jack's pet bear. The caption at the bottom of the photo probably refers to the Seattle, Lakeshore and Eastern railroad which once ran along Lake Washington and through Bothell, now the Burke-Gilman Trail route. Bothell Historical Museum Society. ▼

EAR            NEAR RAILROAD AT BOTHELL

# Mining

▲ Gold prospectors during the Klondike Gold Rush in the Yukon, 1897-1910, used 12-hole crucibles to melt down gold dust and nuggets into rough measured units. Klondike Gold Rush Museum.

◄ The coal miners' safety lamp, ca. 1910, known as a "Davy lamp," was used by the crew chief or fire boss to test air quality in the mine before each shift. If the lamp flared up brightly, it indicated the presence of methane gas; if the flame died down, it meant low oxygen supply and the boss would call for increased fan ventilation. Black Diamond Historical Society.

Seattle's Moran Brothers Company built a dozen shallow-draft steamers for use on the Yukon River during the Klondike Gold Rush. Robert Moran personally escorted the twelve boats from Seattle to the mouth of the Yukon River. The 1898 log book gives the day-to-day details of the hazardous 3000-mile trip. Klondike Gold Rush Museum. ▶

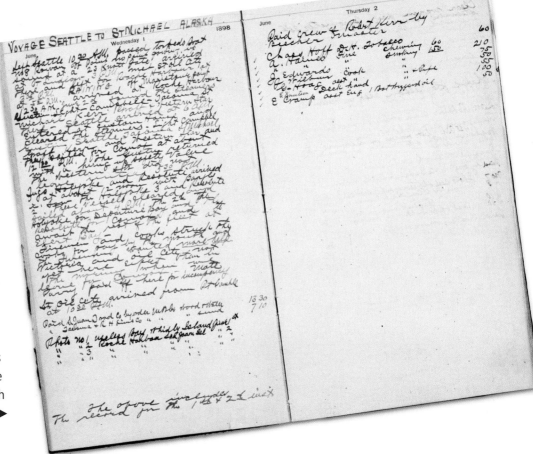

Found by Jack Kombol near Franklin where mines had been operated by the Pacific Coast Coal Company, the 1915 coal miner danger sign in 16 languages documents the diverse nationalities of miners. Many could not read nor speak English. Danger signs such as these were the brainchild of J.W. Stonehouse, who lobbied for standardized safety codes in mines and whose company, Stonehouse Signs of Colorado, began the accident-prevention sign business. In 1912, Stonehouse Signs became one of five founding member companies of what is now known as the National Safety Council. The "Danger Sign" logo was copyrighted in 1914 and the languages section was copyrighted in 1915. Black Diamond Historical Society. ▶

▲ Asahel Curtis' photo documents the Coal Creek Mine near Newcastle and its crew of miners and other employees in 1909. Washington State Historical Society.

# Maritime

▲ The sailing schooner *Wawona* was launched in 1897 at the Bendixsen shipyard in Fairhaven, California – the largest three-masted schooner ever built on the west coast of North America. The ship originally carried lumber but after 1914 was used as a fishing schooner.

The *Wawona's* cod-fishing crew, of about 36 men, shown here ca. 1930, spent six months of each year in the icy Bering Sea. To this day the *Wawona* holds the record for the most cod caught in a single fishing season. The *Wawona*, dismantled in 2009, was listed on the National Register of Historic Places in 1970. Details of the riggings and hold demonstrate its historic seaworthiness. Northwest Seaport images. ▶

Photographs of the *Wawona* prior to being dismantled. Northwest Seaport.

A yearbook published by the Port of Seattle captures the growth and history of Seattle's maritime industry "as it's happening." Washington State Archives. ▶

The Lake Washington Shipyards are depicted here in a 1945 brochure created as part of the shipyard-disposal process by the War Assets Administration at the war's end and included in the Real Property Case File. Today, this site includes the multi-use development of Carillon Point. National Archives and Records Administration. ▼

PROPERTY OF DEFENSE PLANT CORPORATION
A SUBSIDIARY OF RECONSTRUCTION FINANCE CORPORATION

BUILDING WAY NO. 5 AND CRANEWAY NO. 4

The Lake Washington Shipyards were mobilized for production for the U.S. Navy during World War II, building submarine-net tenders and seaplane tenders, as well as repairing warships for both the U.S. and Allies. This photo demonstrates the size of the Kirkland site, which employed more than 8,000 workers. Museum of History & Industry. ▶

The battleship *Nebraska* was launched at Moran Brothers shipyard in 1904. In 1900, Seattle's Moran Brothers Company entered the national shipbuilding field by submitting a bid for the construction of the first-class battleship. When the bids were opened, the Secretary of the Navy announced that all bids were too high. Robert Moran briefed The *Seattle Times* and The *Seattle Post-Intelligencer*, and a whirlwind campaign to raise the $100,000 was launched the next morning to compensate Moran Brothers so that the shipyard could lower its bid. Local sponsors contributed the sum, deposited with the Chamber of Commerce, and the building of the first battleship ever launched from a Puget Sound shipyard was underway.  Costing nearly $4 million, the *Nebraska* was the first U.S.  ▲ battleship built on the Pacific Coast north of San Francisco. The ship's construction had employed 500 workers, and signaled Seattle's entry into steel shipbuilding. The *Nebraska* was launched on October 7, 1904 before  a huge crowd. Puget Sound Maritime Historical Society.

# Manufacturing

A glimpse of the prosperous Crescent Manufacturing Company plant, shown here in 1920. Crescent began as a small spice business at the foot of Seneca Street in 1888, manufacturing baking powder and extracts. Like many Seattle businesses, Crescent was adversely affected by the Great Fire of 1889 and the long national recession which followed.  After the discovery of Klondike gold in 1897, Seattle became the outfitting center and the jumping-off point to the far north, and Crescent grew and prospered with other local businesses over the next decade. It was one of the largest tea, coffee, baking powder and extracts manufacturers on the Pacific Coast.  In 1989, the retail spice business of Crescent Foods was purchased by McCormick and Company.  Seattle Municipal Archives. ▼

BREW

A. HEMRICH Preside
E. F. SWEENEY, Vice Pres

SEA
AND

CABLE ADDRESS
"RAINIER"

Mr. L. Smith, Co

City.

Dear Sir:-

Herewith pe

You will note th

everyone is in f

BOTTLERS OF RAINIER BEER

LE BREWING
TING COMPANY

CHARLES W. LOOMIS, Secretary.
JOHN T. CAMPION, Treasurer.

OWNING & OPERATING
THE BAY VIEW,
SWEENEY & BRAUN
BREWERIES

SEATTLE
BREWING & MALTING
COMPANY.

Seattle, Wash., 6/14/4

mmissioner,

for license for vicinity of Sclus Crik.

Allen Shingle Co. have signed this and

it, with the exception of one of

◄ The Seattle Brewing and Malting Company, as shown on the letterhead, were the brewers of Rainier Beer, and sent various petitions regarding liquor licensing. One letter is to Mr. L. Smith, County Commissioner, on June 6, 1904, while another dated April 1909, remits the license fee and requests the license, signed by brewery cashier C.A. Thorndike. King County Archives liquor license files include applications, correspondence, protests, and petitions for and against the issuance of county licenses for saloons and billiard halls up to the time of the local option prohibition. This series also includes letters of recommendation from breweries and a list of saloons in the county whose license fees were partially refunded when Prohibition took effect in 1912. King County Archives. ▼

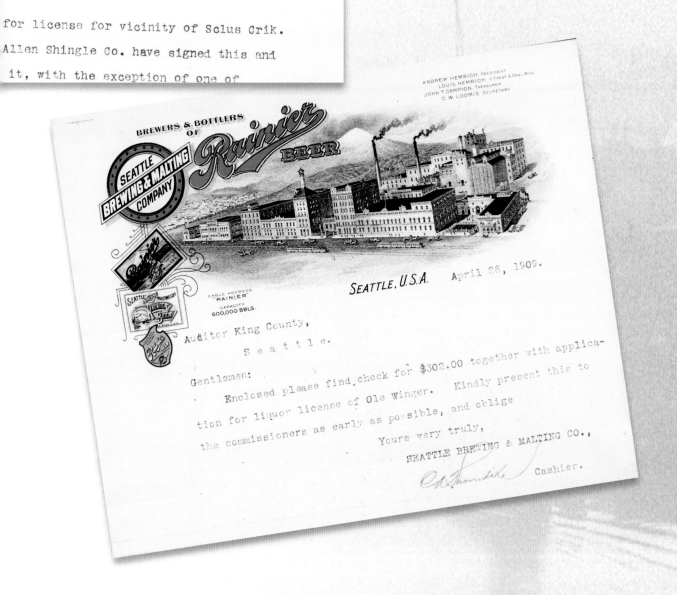

ANDREW HEMRICH, PRESIDENT.
LOUIS HEMRICH, V.PREST & GENL MGR.
JOHN T. CAMPION, TREASURER.
C. W. LOOMIS, SECRETARY.

BREWERS & BOTTLERS OF Rainier BEER

SEATTLE BREWING & MALTING COMPANY

CABLE ADDRESS "RAINIER"
CAPACITY 600,000 BBLS.

SEATTLE, U.S.A.    April 28, 1909.

Auditor King County,
        Seattle.

Gentlemen:

Enclosed please find check for $302.00 together with application for liquor license of Ole Winger. Kindly present this to the commissioners as early as possible, and oblige

Yours very truly,

SEATTLE BREWING & MALTING CO.,

Cashier.

The Walker Trunk Company, conveniently located across the street from the Richmond Beach train depot for shipping of its merchandise, manufactured after-market trunks for Model-T cars, which were initially sold without built-in storage. The nameplate, ca. 1924, denotes the style of trunk on which it was once attached.  Shoreline Historical Museum.  ▶

◀ Sunny Jim peanut butter was manufactured in Seattle by the Pacific Standard Foods company. The company was started in a garage by Germanus Wilhelm Firnstahl, who modeled the rosy-cheeked character after his son, Lowell. During the 1950s the brand accounted for nearly a third of all peanut butter sold in the Seattle area. The large sign on the factory building made the Sunny Jim building on Airport Way South a familiar landmark to passing motorists. In 1997, there was a fire at the plant which destroyed the sign and a portion of the building. On September 20, 2010, a massive fire finished off the Sunny Jim plant as well as a vacant building on the factory site. Museum of History & Industry.

Located in Rainier Valley, Hitt Fireworks was a world-renowned fireworks manufacturer that was started in 1905 by Thomas Gabriel Hitt. The company's name was formalized in 1913. The promotional brochure, ca. 1915, demonstrates their professional approach. Their credits included displays for the 1909 Alaska-Yukon-Pacific Exposition, the Queen of England, and many 4th of July celebrations. Hitt Fireworks also rigged special effects for movies such as "Gone With the Wind." Rainier Valley Historical Society. ▼

◄ The Younger Mints candy tin documents Charles Younger's Bellevue candy manufacturing business, which ran from 1926-1947. Wartime sugar rationing forced him to curtail his operations and eventually sell his business. Eastside Heritage Center.

# chapter ten

# Having Fun

*by Paula Becker*

Having fun – free fun, paid fun, fun celebrated in sunshine or extracted despite showers – created memories of life's lighter moments in King County, Washington.  Local residents found fun in dance halls, parks, roller rinks, and sporting events, at the zoo and at parades, dressed up festively for parties or stripped down to their skivvies at the beach.  They enjoyed these moments with one (or many) friends, with family, neighbors, and communities.  They traveled to wherever fun was happening: on foot, by streetcar, and eventually in automobiles.  As they played, their fun was captured on film and made concrete by the prizes and programs they carried home at day's end, tired and happy.

Examining the photographs, it is impossible not to know that the moments they document were special, gleefully enjoyed, thought about again and again. Having fun was fun, of course, but remembering it went beyond that, affording pleasure, comfort, satisfaction, even solace. Fun was ephemeral, as all fun is – but, saved, the pictures taken and programs detailing those days become documentary evidence, offering the stories of many blissful moments. Discovering the fun King County residents made, had, and remembered offers us a peep-hole into the past, a touchstone that brings us closer to understanding their world – the world that grew into the world we know.

Fun promised respite, rejuvenation, relaxation, a change of pace.  People who used real horses every day still paid to ride the Looff carousel at Luna Park, mounting the intricately carved steeds and reveling in their mechanical gallop.  The busy mother stealing an afternoon from her endless round of stirring, scrubbing, and tending children might

◄ By 1880, well-to-do settlers in Washington Territory could hire dressmakers to design, sew and fit their clothing, and the owner of this ca. 1880 party dress may have done so. However, many women continued to pride themselves on their skills, and sewed clothing for themselves and their families. Daughters of the Pioneers of Washington State.

The unusual "Umbrella Seat" in Kinnear Park was a popular photographic subject, as shown on a February 1907-postmarked card mailed to Montana. Published by the well-known postcard maker Edward H. Mitchell of San Francisco, the card shows the early park feature at a time when the Queen Anne neighborhood was becoming a desirable place to live. Queen Anne Historical Society. ▼

Umbrella seat, Kinnear Park, Seattle

find fun in a blissful hour of stillness spent admiring Puget Sound. For her children, accustomed to filling long summer afternoons with adventures of their own making, having fun could have meant handing over the nickel that allowed them access to whirling, bouncing, shriek-inducing amusement park rides, propelled into an adventure of someone else's making.

Images let us join this fun, and they pose questions. Children clap and crane to watch as their friend dashes, grinning but cautious, balancing his basket of eggs in a race at a Japanese community picnic. Did his brother snap the shutter on a Kodak Brownie camera? Was it developed at Roman's Photographic Company in the Colman Building in downtown Seattle? How did the picture make its way into the archives at the Seattle Buddhist Temple, long after the racer's pounding little feet were still?

Teenaged girls smile gamely, their arms upraised as if to dive, their clinging woolen bathing costumes managing to appear both bold and modest, willing mermaids with a bearded King Neptune, advertising the Alki Natatorium – and inviting us back. Was it the beauty in the middle who tucked the snapshot, and the memory, away in a box on her dresser? Was it her daughter who found it decades later and saved it all her life? Did a granddaughter donate it to the Southwest Seattle Historical Society, in whose archives it has been preserved?

However it was that these treasures arrived at the King County heritage organizations now charged with their care, each photograph, menu, candy tin, and dance card unfolds its own unique story of someone's very special fun, not so long ago.

▲ The caption on this May 25, 1905, dance card from Stockade Hotel at Alki reads: "Solid Comfort at "The Stockade" Grand Opening Ball." The Stockade Hotel was self-proclaimed to be "one of the finest summer hotels in the Pacific Northwest." Alki Point was a community of resorts and vacation homes catering to well-to-do Seattle residents, and viewed itself as a distinct community separate from the City of West Seattle. The hotel served as the polling place for Alki residents when annexation elections to West Seattle were held on October 6, 1906, and May 25, 1907. Southwest Seattle Historical Society.

Lake Washington was a popular vacation spot for Seattleites and visitors, as this ca. 1900 photo of bathing beauties at Brighton Beach can attest.  Rainier Valley Historical Society.  ▼

▲ Pleasure boating on the upper Duwamish River, as shown here in 1909, was a pastime enjoyed by residents of the area. The lower Duwamish River, however,  was dredged and straightened around 1913 to become an industrial channel for Seattle, emptying into Elliott Bay at Harbor Island. Tukwila Historical Society.

*Paula Becker is a staff historian for HistoryLink.org, where her essays document the dance marathon craze of the 1920s and 1930s, war-effort knitting on the home front during World Wars I and II, and the career of* The Egg and I *author Betty MacDonald, among numerous other subjects. She co-wrote (with Alan J. Stein) the books* Alaska-Yukon-Pacific Exposition: Washington's First World's Fair *and* The Future Remembered: the 1962 Seattle World's Fair and Its Legacy, *and she contributed to the book* Knitting America.

▲ With the ferry to Leschi in the background, children Phyllis Hill and Ted McCreary swim, ca. 1920, at Rogers Beach on Lake Washington, located at about 96th Avenue NE, west of Eitel's Beach in Meydenbauer Bay. Eastside Heritage Center.

▲ Luna Park operated from 1907-1913 on the northern tip of Alki Beach in West Seattle. Billed as the "Greatest Amusement Park on the West Coast," the park borrowed its name from Coney Island's Luna Park. It was easily accessible by electric trolley, and drew huge crowds. Major attractions were the Natatorium and the rides, including the roller coaster and the carousel, shown here in 1907. Seattle Municipal Archives.

▲ Angle Lake Park in what is now the SeaTac area opened to recreation in about 1920, eagerly anticipated by waiting bathers. Highline Historical Society.

Fortuna Park on Mercer Island, shown here in about 1910, was a lakeside playground featuring a bathing beach, picnic grounds, playfields and a bandstand. One way of getting there was by passenger ferry, which served not only Mercer Island, but many of the communities around Lake Washington. Principal operator John Anderson of the Anderson Shipyards in Houghton had at least nine steamers plying the lake's waters, one of which was named *Fortuna*. By 1911, boats were regularly serving Medina, Factoria, Kennydale, Beaux Arts, Cozy Cove, Wilburton, Wildwood Park, Atlanta Park and Fortuna Park. A line ran from the end of Seattle's Madison Street to Houghton, Kirkland and Juanita on the east side of the lake. Ferries also steamed from landings in Madrona and Leschi to docks on Mercer Island and Meydenbauer Bay, Mercer Slough and Newcastle Landing. Mercer Island Historical Society. ▼

▲ The winter of the "Big Snow" in the Puget Sound area resulted in many people recording the event. The horse-drawn sleigh at Cedar Falls in 1916 presented an opportunity that the unknown photographer couldn't pass up. Snoqualmie Valley Historical Society.

In 1920, a new football stadium opened at the University of Washington. The UW team played Dartmouth, documented by the program, in the first game held in the stadium, dubbed Washington Field. The East Coast team won the game 28-7. University of Washington Libraries. ▶

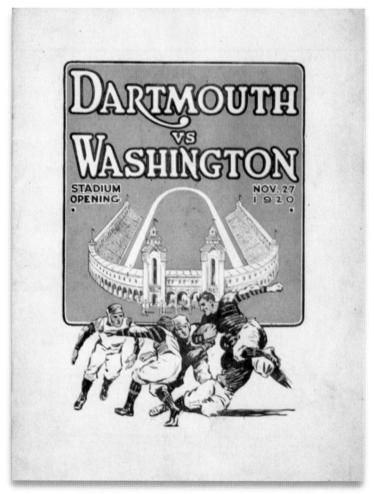

▲ Dressed in Western-style clothing, Japanese American girls were snapped as they take off from the start line in a three-legged race at a Japanese community club picnic in the summer of 1918. Seattle Buddhist Temple.

◄ Built by George Pocock in 1930, the practice shell also known as a wherry, for competitive rowing, is made of Western Red Cedar. George Pocock apprenticed with his father, head boat builder at Eton on the River Thames, in England. He was enticed to Seattle by the first crew coach at the University of Washington, where he set up a shop building boats. The Center for Wooden Boats.

▲ Playland opened in May of 1930, a 12-acre amusement park along the shores of Bitter Lake, accessible by the Interurban. Along with the roller coaster known as the Dipper and a dark ride called the Old Mill, the Fun House was a major attraction complete with trick mirrors, a spinning disc, and a revolving barrel that was best negotiated by crawling on all fours. Shoreline Historical Museum.

There are many stories about the Jolly Roger roadhouse, early menu shown here. While there were illicit establishments that flaunted their disobedience of Prohibition, the Jolly Roger was not among them. It did not open until 1934, a few months after the repeal of the ill-fated law in 1933. The Jolly Roger was a fixture on Lake City Way in North Seattle, and was listed as a Seattle Historic Landmark in 1979. Shoreline Historical Museum. ▶

Clubs and roadhouses, such as the Plantation on Bothell Way in what is now Lake Forest Park, sprang up in the outlying areas along the major highways. The repeal of Prohibition in 1933 allowed nightlife to flourish more openly. The menu is from 1935. Washington State Historical Society. ▼

▲ Shown in some local parade, or perhaps just as an advertising gimmick, Alki Natatorium promoters drive a truck disguised as a parade float, ca. 1935. The publicity was on behalf of what was the third natatorium, which was a heated saltwater swimming pool that opened in 1934, on Alki Beach. Southwest Seattle Historical Society.

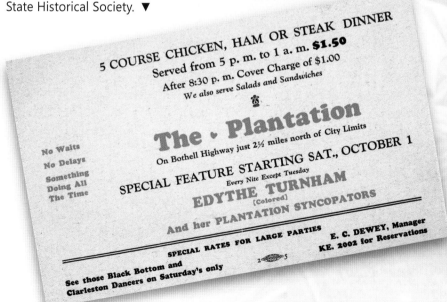

5 COURSE CHICKEN, HAM OR STEAK DINNER
Served from 5 p. m. to 1 a. m. **$1.50**
After 8:30 p. m. Cover Charge of $1.00
*We also serve Salads and Sandwiches*

**The • Plantation**
On Bothell Highway just 2½ miles north of City Limits

No Waits
No Delays
Something
Doing All
The Time

SPECIAL FEATURE STARTING SAT., OCTOBER 1
*Every Nite Except Tuesday*
**EDYTHE TURNHAM**
[Colored]
And her PLANTATION SYNCOPATORS

SPECIAL RATES FOR LARGE PARTIES          E. C. DEWEY, Manager
                                          KE. 2002 for Reservations

See those Black Bottom and
Clarleston Dancers on Saturday's only

▲ In the Americanization of the Nisei (second-generation Japanese Americans), sports played a vital part. Games were played at Seattle Parks Department playfields. Less than two years after this 1940 photo was taken, all residents of Japanese descent were transported inland to World War II internment camps. Seattle Buddhist Temple.

This ca. 1950 promotional brochure features the Federal Shopping Way "Old Line Historic Park." Jack Cissna had a vision of combining shopping with an amusement center for "shopper extras" that would attract families to the shopping center. It never came to fruition because of money and litigation problems. Historical Society of Federal Way. ▶

Two of Many **"Magnetic Attractions"** That Give to Federal Shopping Way Customers "Shopper Extras"

BEARDSLEY, BRAUNER & ROSS
Architects

OLD LINE HISTORIC PARK
FEDERAL SHOPPING WAY

◀ Juanita Beach Park was established in the early 1900s as a privately owned, popular destination beach resort for Seattle-area families. King County acquired the property for the park in 1956, the year the photo was taken. In 2002, the county park was transferred to the City of Kirkland. The King County Parks System photograph collection visually documents park and recreation facilities and programs in King County from 1948 to 1998. King County Archives.

Sewn by the Mutual Helpers of the Richmond Beach Congregational Church between 1936 and 1938, the pansy name quilt was a fundraiser for the church, with 210 people paying to have their names embroidered on it. The quilt was then presented to Mrs. Lena Voreis who was the oldest living charter member of the church. Shoreline Historical Museum. ▶

# chapter eleven

# Arts & Culture

*by Jim Kelly*

You don't think of heritage museums as repositories of great art. They are. Some obvious examples are Nordic Heritage Museum and the Wing Luke Asian Museum, which in addition to having exhibits documenting the experiences of early Nordic and Asian immigrants, also have an array of fine art and crafts representing the best expressions of their respective cultural traditions.

Other heritage museums have fine examples of art within their collections that are overlooked because they are exhibited in the context of history. This point was driven home to me several years ago when I managed the King County Arts Commission Cultural Facilities Program and received a grant application from the White River Valley Museum (WRVM) for funding through the arts program. I thought of White River Valley Museum as a heritage organization, interpreting the rich agricultural history of South King County. With some skepticism that WRVM would be able to make that case that it had an arts component, I nevertheless scheduled Patricia Cosgrove, the museum director, to attend the Arts Cultural Facilities panel review.

She arrived with two objects: a finely woven Native American basket and a child's bonnet, intricately embroidered with beautiful tiny mice trimming the brim. She said, "If this basket and bonnet were displayed in the Seattle Art Museum, you would have no doubt that they are fine works of art. But because they are in a heritage museum, they are considered artifacts. I submit that the WRVM collection reflects elements of heritage and art." The panel agreed and awarded WRVM

▲ Made of natural-white muslin with red triangles and pink cotton binding, the feather-star pattern quilt was pieced by Mrs. David Neely in 1854 as she and her husband crossed the plains by ox team on the Oregon Trail. Eastside Heritage Center.

◄ Emily Inez Denny painted the Battle of Seattle in 1885, nearly 30 years after its occurrence. The painting depicts the settlers of Seattle running to the North Blockhouse on January 26, 1856. A group of about 700 Native warriors had gathered in the woods east of town, and were poised for attack. The U.S. Sloop-of-War *Decatur* is at anchor in Elliott Bay, preparing to fire its cannons. Denny included herself, lower right, as a toddler in her mother's arms. Museum of History & Industry.

▲ Emily Inez Denny's painting, ca. 1880, of Smith Cove is focused on a white farmhouse and outbuildings flanked by dense forest, the home of Dr. Henry A. Smith. A man and woman stand in the clear-cut foreground surveying the cove and Elliott Bay. Denny, the daughter of pioneers David and Louisa Boren Denny, painted a number of historic subjects, and documented pioneer stories in published works. Museum of History & Industry.

funds from the arts program. I have been fascinated with the breadth of "heritage" collections ever since.

Seattle has always been at the intersection of world cultures and its art has reflected the traditions of its diverse populations, as evidenced in the images in this chapter. These paintings, photographs, sculptures, playbills, quilts and other artworks and documents are housed in heritage collections across the county. They are evidence that heritage museums collect art.

Thanks to the dedicated work of heritage professionals, we are able to track the development of the arts in our region. The 1962 World's Fair, which in its aftermath launched Seattle Repertory Theatre, followed by Seattle Opera (1963), A Contemporary Theatre (1965) and Pacific Northwest Ballet (1972), is often credited as the event that began the transformation of Seattle from a cultural "backwater" to a sophisticated modern city. "Backwater" is too strong a word. Prior to 1962 Seattle lacked the institutional arts, but it didn't lack for vocational or avocational arts or opportunities to experience high-quality cultural presentations. Seattle and its early settlers always had a thirst for art and cultural entertainment.

Consider that on March 15, 1875, a mere 23 years after the Denny Party landed at Alki Point, the Fanny Morgan Phelps Company performed *The Taming of the Shrew,* the first Shakespearean play ever produced on a Seattle stage, at Yesler's Hall on First and Cherry.

Four years later, on November 24, 1879, Seattle's first real theatre – Squires Opera House –opened on the east side of First Avenue (then Commercial Street) between Washington and Main. With 584 seats on two levels, this venue could house operas, plays, music concerts, and minstrel acts.

Here's the surprise that speaks either to the optimism of the building's owners or the demand for entertainment from the populace: according to the U.S. Census, in 1880, just after the performance hall opened, Seattle had a population of only 3,553. The theatre was not

▲ Lorinda Hopkins Scammon and her husband Isaiah L. Scammon homesteaded in Montesano, January 18, 1853. She made the "crazy quilt," around 1888 and gave it to her granddaughter Juanita Edwards Johnson. Daughters of the Pioneers of Washington State.

◄ The 1918 symphony harp-guitar was played by Joseph M. Smith, who performed with Wagner's Band and for several theaters in Seattle, including playing accompaniment in the Dreamland Theater during the silent picture days. Smith was from Bangor, Maine and arrived in Seattle just before the great fire in 1889. He was a member of the local Musicians Union for many years. Pioneer Association of the State of Washington.

▲ Documentation of Welsh cultural festivals and competitions celebrating music and poetry in King County can be found as early as 1890. The 1909 Alaska-Yukon-Pacific Eisteddfod Association of Seattle was sponsored by Welsh boosters from all parts of Washington and Oregon. The competition was held in the Exposition Auditorium, August 27 and 28, 1909. The caption on the brochure, "Mor o gan yw Cymru i gyd" – translates to "Wales is a sea of song." Fifty-three years later, the 6th Regional Welsh "Gymanfa Ganu," a "singing festival," was held in conjunction with the Seattle World's Fair, June 28 through July 1, 1962. Puget Sound Welsh Association.

profitable, for reasons that should be readily apparent, and three years later, the owners turned it into the New Brunswick Hotel.

In 1890, Ladies Musical Club was founded with the purpose of stimulating the development of musical activity in what was then still a frontier community. LMC inaugurated a concert series presenting great visiting artists over a period of decades that reads like a Who's Who of musical history: Pablo Casals, Marilyn Horne, Paderewski, Rachmaninoff, Arthur Rubinstein and more.

Seattle Symphony presented its first performance on December 29, 1903. Its move to Benaroya Hall in September of 1998 was the culmination of almost 100 years of symphonic success.

The Seattle Art Museum tracks its roots to the 1906 formation of the Seattle Fine Arts Society. It wasn't until 1931 that Dr. Richard E. Fuller forged a partnership with the City of Seattle, donating funds and much of his personal collection of Chinese and Japanese art to create the Seattle Art Museum in Volunteer Park, which opened in 1933 and drew 300,000 visitors in its first six months. Today Seattle Art Museum is one of the great visual art museums in the United States. It operates three venues: the downtown Seattle Art Museum, Olympic Sculpture Park, and the Seattle Asian Art Museum, in the 1933 Carl Gould-designed Art Deco facility that was SAM's original home.

In 1914, Nellie Cornish, former unpaid music teacher in the local high school in Blaine, Washington, founded Cornish School of Music. With a philosophy of teaching music in relation to all other art forms, she soon added dance and visual art, followed by theatre and design. Within

▲ The Northern Clay Company sketchbook contains addresses, notes, expenses, and drawings for terracotta sculptures dating from 1910 to 1926. It belonged to Louis Shubert, head sculptor at the Northern Clay Terracotta Plant. The Auburn company manufactured architectural terracotta features that decorated many Pacific Northwest buildings. In 1925, Gladding McBean, a large clay company from California, acquired the Northern Clay Company. The name was changed to Gladding McBean & Co. in 1927. The plant operated from 1910 to 1932 and was a major employer in the area until the Great Depression forced the company to close its local terracotta division and consolidate its other various local operations. White River Valley Museum.

Louis Shubert, photographed working on a terracotta design, was the head sculptor at the Northern Clay Company and Gladding McBean & Co. from 1922-1932. White River Valley Museum. ▶

three years Cornish College had enrolled over 600
students and was the largest music school west of
Chicago, developing the blueprint for what would
become today's Cornish College of the Arts, one
of the premier arts schools in the country and one
of a few with programs in every artistic discipline.

People of all cultures and throughout time have
created art to document historic events, interpret
or re-imagine their world, express their personal
thoughts, feelings and points of view, delight,
entertain, challenge and celebrate. Artists and the
products of the creative process share something in
common with heritage specialists and the collections
they steward: they remind us who we are and where
we've come from, celebrating both the diversity
and the universality of the human experience.

---

*Jim Kelly has been the Executive Director of 4Culture,
the cultural development authority of King County,
since 2003. Jim became the Associate Director of
the King County Arts Commission in 1995, and
then Manager of the Office of Cultural Resources
in 1998. He moved to Seattle from New York City
in 1991, where he served as the Assistant Director
of the Community Arts Development Program
and later as Director of Real Estate Services for
the city's Department of Cultural Affairs.*

◄ Incorporated by Martin Beck in 1919, The Orpheum Theater, built in 1911, was located at Third Avenue and Madison Street in Seattle, and was part of the Orpheum Circuit which operated 45 vaudeville theatres located in 36 cities throughout the United States and Canada. The program is from December 12, 1925. A new Orpheum Theater opened in Seattle at Fifth Avenue and Stewart in 1927. University of Washington Libraries.

Ron Upshaw and Don O'Neill, known as "The Ron and Don Duo," provided popular entertainment in the 1920s on the Wurlitzer theater organ at the Paramount. The inscription on the 1928 photo reads: "To our friend and partner in crime, Sandy Balcom, Always Ron and Don." Sandy Balcom owned Balcom & Vaughan Pipe Organs in Seattle. Puget Sound Theatre Organ Society. ▼

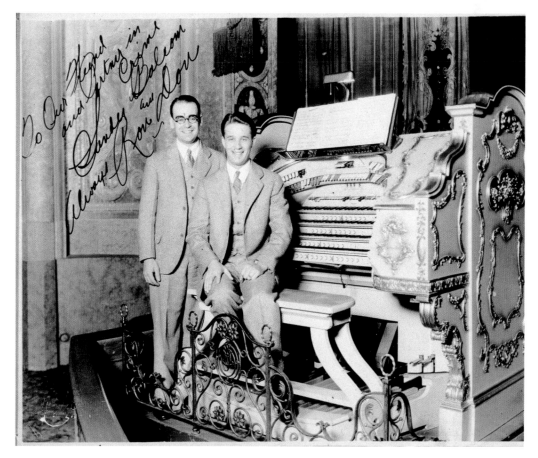

▲ Japanese settlers in and around Seattle traveled to the International District to view traditional Kabuki theater presentations, such as this one from 1928. Washington State Historical Society.

In an undated photo, a Japanese actor costumed as a warrior poses for what is likely a publicity shot. The costuming is typical of a Noh play, classic Japanese musical theater, produced in Seattle's Nihonmachi, or Japantown. Seattle Buddhist Temple. ▶

▲ A 1928 painting by Stewart Swenson provides a view of the Snoqualmie Falls Lumber Company from the middle of the mill pond. The central subject is Mill No. 2, which was engineered to cut Western Red Cedar and Western Hemlock. Mill No. 2 started production on May 24, 1918 and was dismantled in 1960 to 1961. Snoqualmie Valley Historical Society.

Renowned artist Richard Bennett was a significant part of the rich "Northwest School" arts scene with such notables as Morris Graves, Mark Tobey, Kenneth Callahan and Guy Anderson. Bennett illustrated over 200 books, and documented numerous Northwest scenes, such as Lake Union, shown here in his 1931 publication *Puget Sound Woodcuts*, with text by Glenn Hughes. University of Washington Libraries. ▶

LAKE UNION, SEATTLE

Artist Eustace Ziegler had long advocated government funding for the arts. As a show of support for the first New Deal arts program, called the Public Works of Art Project (PWAP), Ziegler donated his 1937 painting *Mt. Index,* for placement in a non-profit agency. Mt. Index was painted on the back of another painting, painfully demonstrating that Ziegler himself suffered the economic hardships of the Great Depression and frugally reused materials where he could. Museum of History & Industry. ▶

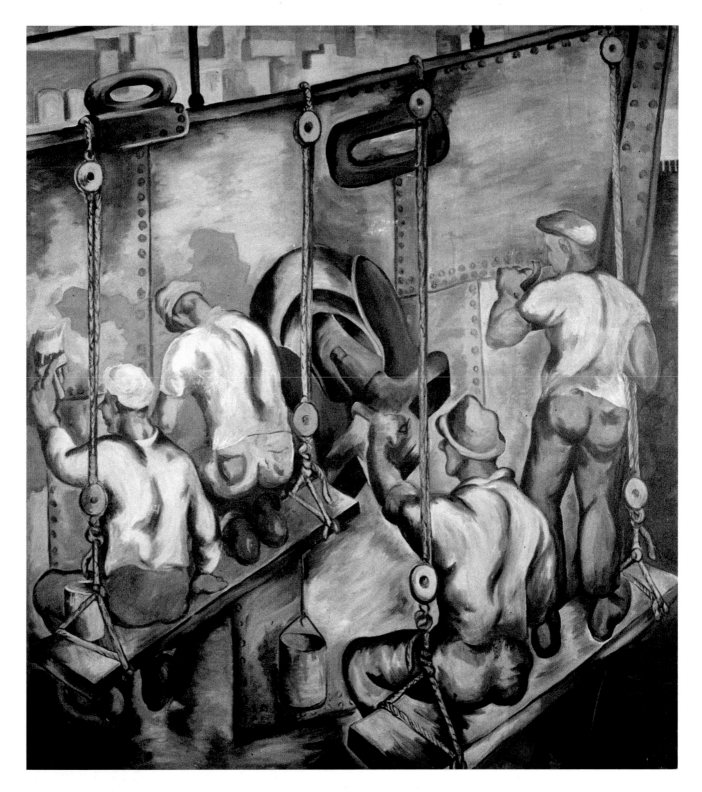

▲ Kenneth Callahan was commissioned by the Federal Art Project to produce the 1936 *Men Who Work the Ships*. Seen here is a panel from the larger multi-paneled mural painted for the Seattle Marine Hospital. The Federal Art Project was one of several Depression-era programs designed to put people to work. Many artists benefited from the program, as did the viewing public. Callahan painted several such murals as part of the project. Museum of History & Industry.

Glenn Hughes, director of the University of Washington's Showboat Theatre, received an urgent telegram from writer Helen Robinson of *LIFE* Magazine on May 19, 1939, requesting additional information to run with photos of the theater in the following week's issue. University of Washington Libraries. ▶

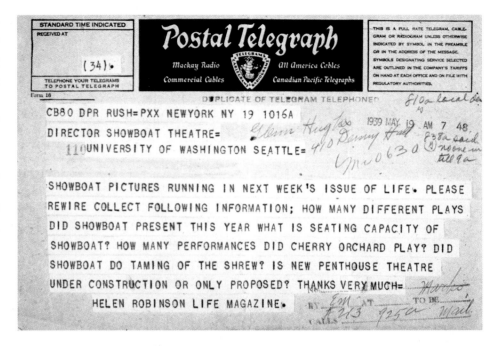

STANDARD TIME INDICATED
RECEIVED AT

(34).

TELEPHONE YOUR TELEGRAMS
TO POSTAL TELEGRAPH

Form 16

## Postal Telegraph

Mackay Radio
Commercial Cables
All America Cables
Canadian Pacific Telegraphs

THIS IS A FULL RATE TELEGRAM, CABLE-GRAM OR RADIOGRAM UNLESS OTHERWISE INDICATED BY SYMBOL IN THE PREAMBLE OR IN THE ADDRESS OF THE MESSAGE. SYMBOLS DESIGNATING SERVICE SELECTED ARE OUTLINED IN THE COMPANY'S TARIFFS ON HAND AT EACH OFFICE AND ON FILE WITH REGULATORY AUTHORITIES.

DUPLICATE OF TELEGRAM TELEPHONED

CB80 DPR RUSH=PXX NEWYORK NY 19 1016A

DIRECTOR SHOWBOAT THEATRE=

110UNIVERSITY OF WASHINGTON SEATTLE=

SHOWBOAT PICTURES RUNNING IN NEXT WEEK'S ISSUE OF LIFE. PLEASE REWIRE COLLECT FOLLOWING INFORMATION; HOW MANY DIFFERENT PLAYS DID SHOWBOAT PRESENT THIS YEAR WHAT IS SEATING CAPACITY OF SHOWBOAT? HOW MANY PERFORMANCES DID CHERRY ORCHARD PLAY? DID SHOWBOAT DO TAMING OF THE SHREW? IS NEW PENTHOUSE THEATRE UNDER CONSTRUCTION OR ONLY PROPOSED? THANKS VERY MUCH=

HELEN ROBINSON LIFE MAGAZINE.

H. Hagiya

▲ Artist Hisashi Hagiya, confined to Camp Minidoka in Hunt, Idaho during the Japanese internment, painted his impressions of the place. He worked in the sign shop at Minidoka. Born in Japan, Hagiya came to Seattle around 1920 and attended Cornish Art School. Seattle Buddhist Temple.

Commissioned in 1949 to create a sculpture to be added to the World War II Memorial at Seattle's Public Safety building, Dudley Pratt produced the touching *Gold Star Mother*, the plaster model of which is shown here. The resulting sculpture was placed in 1952 above the list of war dead carved in granite, where it remained until the Public Safety building was razed. The sculpture is now loaned to Evergreen Washelli for the Veterans' Memorial Cemetery.  Museum of History & Industry.  ▶

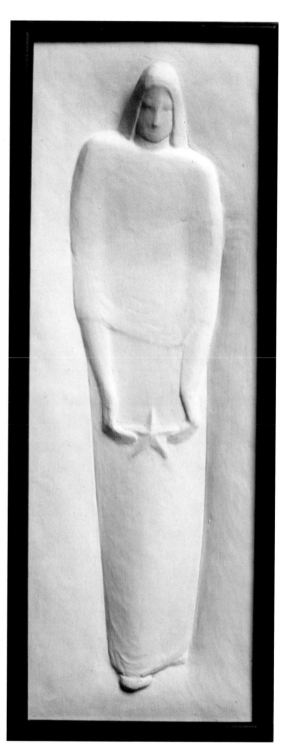

▲ Dubbed "the Pearl of the North" by Northwest artist friends, Helmi Juvonen (1903-1985) was a prolific artist who went largely unrecognized until later in her troubled life. She was born in Montana to Finnish parents, who moved to Seattle when Helmi was 15. She attended the Cornish School of the Arts in Seattle and learned various aspects of art from such people as Jacob Elshin and Richard Odlin. Her interest in Northwest Native American culture led to acquaintances with local Native Americans, and she created numerous studies of Native American ceremonies and practices. The untitled and undated sculpture shown here demonstrates her depth and feeling, and her impressive artistic ability. Nordic Heritage Museum.

# chapter twelve

# In a Broader Context

*by Charles Payton*

The King County region has developed a unique relationship to the United States and the world based upon its location, resources and ingenuity.

Native Americans migrated into what is now King County thousands of years ago, establishing villages along the waterways. Even before the County was established, the region was shaped politically and demographically by Euro-American powers and treaties, as well as introduced diseases that swept across the continent.

By the time King County became part of the newly formed Washington Territory in 1853, settlers had already been staking claims on traditional Indian lands under the federal Oregon Donation Land Act. Treaties with the Tribes were hastily drawn up in the mid-1850s, but even so, the tensions turned into hostilities. It took over a century and a federal lawsuit, *U.S. v. Washington*, the "Boldt Decision," to resolve major treaty rights.

King County began its trade with the outside world beginning in the 1850s, with coal, lumber products, produce and salmon among the earliest exports. International trade accelerated in the late 1890s as large-scale commerce with Asian countries was initiated. Before the turn of the 20th century, Washington had already emerged as the nation's foremost producer of forest products, a position it held for almost half a century.

Said to have been sewn from the undergarments of the women barricaded in the North Blockhouse during the Battle of Seattle in 1856, the American "petticoat" flag is made of red wool flannel, white and blue linen, and cotton-print tie tabs. Museum of History & Industry. ▼

▲ The Hudson's Bay Company in Washington Territory was not above trading its goods for items that might be, in turn, traded to someone else. The early-1800s flintlock musket, which was accepted in trade for some commodity on the company shelves, is a prime example of the enterprising nature of Hudson's Bay. The dragon motif suggests that the weapon was originally manufactured for trade in Asia or India. Museum of History & Industry.

The rapid growth of the region's often dangerous and sometimes exploitive industries gave rise to the growth of a number of labor unions. The Knights of Labor, a national organization that began organizing locally in the King County coalfields, was instrumental in fomenting anti-Chinese hysteria in the mid-1880s. Locals of the Industrial Workers of the World (IWW) or "Wobblies," United Mine Workers, Longshoremen, Teamsters, and other unions grew in power in the early 20th century to better the lives of workers, although violent confrontations between management and labor continued here sporadically for decades.

The U.S. acquisition of the Alaska Territory from Russia in 1867 gave rise to one of the region's most enduring economic ties. During the Klondike Gold Rush of 1897, fortunes were made by local entrepreneurs who became producers and provisioners for the gold-seekers, thereby "mining the miners." Subsequent federal legislation helped establish Seattle as a primary shipping hub to Alaska.

The region's first world's fair, the Alaska-Yukon-Pacific Exposition (AYPE) focused international attention on Seattle and King County in 1909, and was a financial success that left a legacy of buildings benefiting the University of Washington. The AYPE emblem: "Orient meets Occident in the Golden West," celebrated the region's rise to prominence as a world trade center.

Federal involvement in the construction of hydroelectric dams along the mighty Columbia River system facilitated industrial development, including aluminum production in the state, an important factor in the growth of the aeronautical industry of King County. The region's strategic location, abundant resources, inexpensive access to hydroelectric power and industrial might have assured it a prominent role in national defense efforts through two world wars and several other conflicts. The numerous facilities established around the region by the Armed Services have played a significant role in the regional economy since the 19th century.

▲ Fred Matthiesen, a Rainier Valley resident, went to the Yukon in 1897 as one of the 10,000 hopeful miners who trekked north that first year of the gold rush. Photographed by a Dawson City studio, Matthiesen and F.F. Coffin display "the largest gold nugget ever discovered" which they found "below Upper Discovery Dominion Creek." Rainier Valley Historical Society.

In March 1886, a mob ▶ led by local representatives of the Knights of Labor rampaged through the streets of Seattle, driving hundreds of local Chinese residents to the waterfront. As the violence escalated, the Home Guard, a vigilante group organized to keep the peace, was called out and martial law declared. The engraving is from *Harper's Weekly* magazine, March 6, 1886. Wing Luke Asian Museum.

THE ANTI-CHINESE RIOT AT SEATTLE, WASHINGTON TERRITORY.—Drawn by W. P. Snyder, from Sketches by J. F. Whiting, of Seattle.—[See Page 155.]
1. Driving Chinamen on Board of the Steamer.　　　2. Marching under Guard to the Court-house.

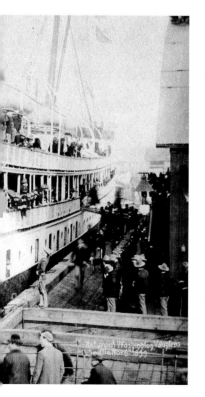

◀ Photographer Anders Beer Wilse was on hand to greet a large group of Washington military volunteers returning to Seattle from the Spanish American War in 1899. Washington State Historical Society.

Immigration from East Asia was severely restricted for many years under U.S. treaties and laws, allowing Asian laborers to work for railroads, canneries, mills and farms, but often preventing permanent Asian settlement and land tenure. The racially motivated restrictions culminated in Executive Order 9066, which in 1942 led to the incarceration in relocation camps of both immigrant Japanese and American citizens of Japanese descent from the West Coast. Significantly, the successful, national movement for redress began here.

In 1916 Washington State banned the sale of alcoholic beverages, and the United States followed with the Volstead Act in 1920, which attempted to enforce nationwide prohibition until its repeal in 1933. An underground economy developed with local rum runners importing liquor from Canada, and stills were set up around King County.

When the disastrous, nationwide Great Depression followed the Wall Street financial collapse in 1929, millions of Americans were destitute. The federal response launched numerous economic, social and public works programs. Prominent among them was the Works Progress (later Projects) Administration or WPA, which employed local workers in a spectrum of occupations from the arts to social services and facility construction. Federal Depression-era programs succeeded in providing a lasting legacy of cultural, economic and infrastructural improvements throughout the region.

America's long march for civil rights began, perhaps, with our Declaration of Independence, Constitution and Bill of Rights, and continues today. Campaigns for civil rights began here before statehood in 1889, and included efforts towards voting rights for women, finally achieved in 1910. Since then, progress has been made in many significant areas, including: open housing; integrated education; equal-employment opportunity; and public accessibility for all citizens.

▲ Commemorating the visit of the Great White Fleet to Seattle, the Navy parades north on Second Avenue in downtown Seattle on May 26, 1908. The festivities are captured for posterity by photographer Asahel Curtis, whose vantage point above the crowd near James Street presents a unique view. Washington State Historical Society.

▲ The "Official Birds Eye View" postcard of the 1909 Alaska-Yukon-Pacific Exposition shows off the Olmsted Brothers' meticulous landscape design for the AYPE, oriented along Rainier Vista toward Mount Rainier. Their plan endures as the University of Washington campus today. In a second postcard, the imagery of a man with dog sled and team meeting a lumberjack suggests one of the overarching themes of the fair: Seattle as a gateway to the rich resources of Alaska and the Yukon. The "Pay Streak" was the Exposition's midway and included carnival rides, exhibits, concessions, and entertainment. University of Washington Libraries.

This region's unique and strategic role within the broader context of national and world affairs has long been recognized. From somewhat insular beginnings in the nation's northwest corner, the King County region has emerged as a powerful incubator of ideas and innovations that have gone national and global, with many creative contributions to the arts, education, business and industry.

*Charles Payton serves on the Washington State Historical Records Advisory Board. A prolific historian with many writings to his credit, he was the administrator of the Heritage Division for King County Cultural Resources from 1985 to 2002, and the staff lead of the Heritage Program for 4Culture from 2002 to 2006.*

◄ Seattle Day was held September 6, 1909, and was one of the dozens of "special day" designations that were assigned for nearly every day of the Alaska-Yukon-Pacific Exposition, which ran from June 1 through October 16, 1909. The Seattle Day ribbon belonged to an early Bellevue family who attended the fair, and brought the ribbon home as a memento.  Eastside Heritage Center.

▲ In the 1910 campaign for women's right to vote in Washington State, suffragists hang "Women Vote" posters with quotes from Abraham Lincoln, Theodore Roosevelt and Mark Twain. Washington State Historical Society.

The Alaska-Yukon-Pacific Exposition was Seattle's first world's fair and every business in town participated in the boosterism and promotion of the event.  Commemorative items such as this plate were typical of the souvenirs available at the fair. Klondike Gold Rush Museum.  ►

The 1911 postcard "Queen of the Poll" lampoons the victory for women's suffrage enacted in 1910 in Washington State. Washington was the fifth state in the U.S. to grant women the right to vote in state, county, and municipal elections. ▶

In 1920, the 19th Amendment to the US Constitution was passed, giving women the right to vote nationally. University of Washington Libraries.

SUFFRAGETTE SERIES Nº 9

VOTE FOR
BILL SYKES
FOR
KEEPER OF THE ZOO

DON'T VOTE FOR
Dr. Mc MONEY
FOR TREASURER
VOTE FOR HIS WIFE
SHE HAS BEEN HIS
TREASURE FOR 40 YRS.

VOTE FOR
SUSIE PEACH
FOR
ALDERWOMAN
5TH WARD.

VOTE FOR
MISS SPINSTER
JUSTICE
CHILDRENS' COURT.

BEFORE VOTING SEE
ANN HOWOLDE
BOODLE-HOLDER
OF THE COMMITTEE
FOR THE EMANCIPATION
OF THE WEAKER SEX
FROM THE OTHER SEX.

JANE DIKKER
FOR
GOVERNESS
OF THE
BLUE-GRASS-WIDOW
STATE.
LADIES, PROVE THAT
YOU ARE MEN.

DISTRICT LEADERESS

QUEEN OF THE POLL.

COPYRIGHTED.

◄ The Industrial Workers of the World (IWW), whose members were known as "Wobblies," was established in Chicago in 1905, and was largely directed by William "Big Bill" Haywood, the head of the Western Federation of Miners. In the west, the IWW appealed to loggers, shingle-mill workers and miners, who often labored long hours in unsafe conditions for substandard pay. The IWW welcomed all workers, including immigrants, minorities and women. By 1912, the IWW claimed 100,000 members, and posters such as the 1911 example here, and the 1919 wood sign, helped spread the word about the union. In 1919, the Wobblies were influential in leading Seattle's General Strike, the first in North America. University of Washington Libraries. ▼

▲ Seattle's Dry Squad, photographed here in 1919, was initially charged with enforcing Washington's law that, beginning in 1916, prohibited alcoholic beverages in the state. However, on the heels of Washington's law came the 18th Amendment which went into effect on January 17, 1920, banning liquor nationally. All law enforcement authorities - federal, state, county, and municipal - were responsible for upholding Prohibition, which did not end until 1933. Seattle Metropolitan Police Museum.

▲ During Prohibition, criminals formed gangs, the better to control the wealth of illegal booze. The Thompson submachine gun, or "Tommy Gun" such as the ca. 1930 model here, became a favorite weapon of organized crime, as well as of those trying to enforce the law. The gun was an "automatic," able to fire a volley of .45 cartridges very rapidly. Seattle Metropolitan Police Museum.

As the Great Depression wore on, many unemployed citizens, often already on society's margins, became homeless. In October 1931, an unemployed lumberjack by the name of Jesse Jackson and twenty others built shacks on vacant land owned by the Port of Seattle a few blocks south of Pioneer Square. They named the shantytown "Hooverville," a sarcastic reference to Herbert Hoover who was president as the Depression began. The population grew quickly. Hooverville's sprawl is evident in photographs such as this. A 1934 census of Hooverville documented 632 men and 7 women living in 479 shanties, with ages ranging from 15 to 73. The shantytown remained in existence until 1941, when a "shack elimination program" was implemented. Washington State Archives. ▼

▲ An enterprising restaurateur set up shop under a railroad bridge in Auburn, documented here in a 1931 photo, as the cook, entrepreneur and customers casually pose in front of the improvised eatery. During the Depression, out-of-work citizens became rail-riding transients looking for any kind of employment, and they often set up camps near railroad tracks. Was the innovator of this cafe a displaced Auburn restaurant owner, or a traveler making good? Notice the stick-built shanty in the far right background. White River Valley Museum.

▲ The first relief office in Seattle, located in Columbia City, was a private effort, inspired by the lack of government response to the joblessness and poverty of the Great Depression. A collaboration between members of some labor unions and members of the Communist Party, the obvious need was documented in the 1932 photo of the funeral-like procession of people waiting for help. Rainier Valley Historical Society.

◄ Seattle Police Detective James Lawrence's 1932 "Revenuer" Badge issued by the U.S. Treasury during Prohibition bears testament to the federal government's tight rein on alcohol. Lawrence was one of the officers responsible for enforcing Prohibition, even as the sentiment by that time throughout the country was toward legalization. Seattle Metropolitan Police Museum.

◄ When the "Noble Experiment" of Prohibition ended on December 5, 1933, some businesses were already poised to get back into alcohol production and consumption, but others worked their way into the industry more gradually. One of Maple Valley's home industries benefited from Prohibition's reversal, that of making wine from apples grown in local orchards. The wine "bottle," designed more like a pint for whiskey, is ca. 1935. Maple Valley Historical Society.

Fay Chong (1912-1973) was born in Kwangtung, China, and came to Seattle with his parents at the age of eight. He attended Broadway High School and the University of Washington, and studied privately with Leon Derbyshire and Mark Tobey. Chong's self-portrait is from 1935, prior to his joining the Federal Art Project in Seattle. He produced numerous works for the project from 1938 to 1942, and eventually was an illustrator for the Boeing Company. He was a significant part of the art scene in the Northwest, founding the Chinese Art Club with Andrew Chinn. He was a member of the Northwest Printmakers, the Northwest Watercolor Society, Puget Sound Group of Northwest Painters and the Washington Art Association. Wing Luke Asian Museum. ▲

▲ Preserved in the Seattle Parks and Recreation's Sherwood History Files, the 1934 photo of Woodland Park demonstrates the important legacy left by Donald N. Sherwood (1916-1981), Parks engineer from 1955 to 1977. Along with designing buildings and producing brochures, Sherwood sketched maps of the parks, made historical comments on them, and even wrote individual histories for nearly every facility. When Sherwood learned that historical department records were being destroyed as employees retired, he advocated for archiving the files, and was awarded the responsibility in 1972. Sherwood continued this work even after his position was eliminated due to a budget reduction in 1977.  Seattle Municipal Archives.

▲ The Works Progress Administration was a program of the New Deal, with multiple purposes. The WPA put unemployed men and women to work in many fields, from designing public art to building public projects that generated hydroelectricity, spanned rivers or built parks, such as seen here in a 1936 photo of a WPA construction project at Seward Park. Seattle Municipal Archives.

The Minidoka Relocation Center was one of the wartime internment camps established for people of Japanese descent, as a result of Executive Order 9066. Camp Minidoka, located in south central Idaho, occupied a 33,000 acre site, included more than 600 buildings, and housed approximately 13,000 internees from Washington, Oregon, and Alaska. It was in operation from August 1942 until October 1945. People were issued some necessities at the camp, such as the Army cot seen here. Wing Luke Asian Museum. ▶

Three youngsters wearing their Camp Fire Girl attire demonstrate for the camera how to work in a 1943 World War II homefront Victory Garden. Camp Fire Museum. ▼

▲ Seattle citizens marched following the assassination of Dr. Martin Luther King, Jr. on April 12, 1968. In the photograph are Rabbi Raphael Levine of Temple DeHirsch, Archbishop Thomas Connolly, and Walter Hubbard, president of the Seattle Black Catholic Lay caucus. Archives of the Archdiocese of Seattle.

# Index of Photos